Decisional
Dialogues
in a
Cultural
Context

Decisional Dialogues in a Cultural Context

Structured Exercises

Paul B. Pedersen & Daniel Hernandez

SAGE Publications
International Educational and Professional Publisher
Thousand Oaks   London   New Delhi

For information address:

 SAGE Publications, Inc.
2455 Teller Road
Thousand Oaks, California 91320
Phone: 805-499-0721
E-mail: order@sagepub.com

SAGE Publications Ltd.
6 Bonhill Street
London EC2A 4PU
United Kingdom

SAGE Publications India Pvt. Ltd.
M-32 Market
Greater Kailash I
New Delhi 110 048 India

Printed in the United States of America

Library of Congress Cataloging-in-Publication Data

Pedersen, Paul, 1936-
    Decisional dialogues in a cultural context: Structured
exercises / Paul B. Pedersen and Daniel Hernandez.
        p.   cm.
    Includes bibliographical references.
    ISBN 0-7619-0303-8 (pbk.: acid-free paper)
    1. Employment interviewing. 2. Decision-making. 3. Diversity in
the workplace. I. Hernandez, Daniel. II. Title.
    HF5549.5.I6P42   1996
    658.3′1124—dc20   96-4429

This book is printed on acid-free paper.

97 98 99 00 01 02 10 9 8 7 6 5 4 3 2 1

Acquiring Editor: Marquita Fleming
Editorial Assitant: Frances Borghi
Production Editor: Sherrise Purdum
Production Assistant: Karen Wiley
Copy Editor: Joyce Kuhn
Typesetter/Designer: Andrea D. Swanson/Ravi Balasuriya
Cover Designer: Ravi Balasuriya

Table of Contents

Introduction

Most decisions in the workplace are based on data collected through interviews. People are hired, fired, evaluated, and promoted based on interview data. Products are bought, sold, traded, or given away based on interview data. Decisional interviewing is different from counseling in that decisional interviewing focus on the task of making a decision *for* or *with* the client and not just to help the client make his or her own decision. Decisional interviewing involves a problem definition phase, a work phase to identify alternatives, and a decision phase to select an alternative.

The decisional interview is more than a conversation; it is a purposive, problem-solving process where data are gathered in a systematic way to make good decisions. Organizations fail or succeed depending on the accuracy of interview data. Decisional interviewing begins with (1) a problem that needs to be solved in some way or a decision that needs to be made. (2) As much data as possible are gathered relevant to that problem or decision. (3) The most promising alternative solutions or decisions are identified and narrowed down in a priority ranking. (4) The "best" solution or decision is then tried out through application to real-world situations. The range of interviewing situations may range from "checking out" a colleague, boss, or employee through informal methods and perhaps in an informal setting to contractual discussions achieved through formal methods in formal settings. Decisional interviewing is defined broadly to include the full range of applications.

Decisional interviewing is a complicated process when it is done well. Many if not most professionals in the workplace have neither read a book on interviewing nor have they been trained for interviewing skills, and yet they are expected to learn on the job how to become expert interviewers. Learning interviewing skills on the job is indeed possible but it can be a very expensive way to learn because people make mistakes.

The most serious mistake that interviewers make is to use the "self-reference criterion," which is to assume that other people are like yourself and can be judged by the same criterion. Culturally encapsulated interviewers are most at risk to project their own perspective on their clients. People are both different and similar. A good decisional interviewer will acknowledge that difference and discover the common-ground similarities.

Putting the decisional interview in a cultural context means (1) increasing the interviewer's multicultural *awareness* of one's own culturally learned underlying assumptions, which are typically unexamined; (2) increasing the interviewer's cultural *knowledge*, information, and—most important of all—accurate comprehension of the client's cultural context and understanding of the "meaning" that context has for the client, and (3) increasing the interviewer's appropriate *skill* for making appropriate changes at the right time in the right way. By increasing cultural awareness, knowledge, and skill the interviewer will comprehend the client's cultural context.

This book focuses on decisional interviewing in a cultural context that recognizes ethnographic, demographic, status, and affiliation differences between people. These broadly defined cultural differences become important because people from different cultural contexts make different assumptions. Structured exercises in this guidebook will present a variety of contrasting cultural contexts. Each cultural context will require a different approach for decisional interviewing if accurate data are desired. Otherwise, the same behavior may have a different meaning, and different behaviors might have the same meaning. The structured exercises provide an opportunity for decisional interviewers to enlarge their repertoire of interviewing styles to fit the range of contrasting cultural contexts in which decisional interviewing is used.

The first part of this book includes a variety of activities usually requiring two or more persons to interact in structured roles from contrasting perspectives. These exercises are divided into three sections. The first set is directed toward increasing the interviewer's multicultural self-awareness of his or her own culturally learned underlying assumptions. The second set is directed toward increasing the interviewer's multicultural knowledge, information, or comprehension of the client's cultural context. The third set is directed toward increasing the interviewer's multicultural skill for making right and appropriate interventions through the interviewing technique.

These three categories provide a preliminary foundation for decisional interviewing in the cultural context and prepare the interviewer to identify and include one's own and the client's cultural context in the interviewing process.

Most of these structured exercises have been used successfully in teaching and training interviewers in the past. Sometimes, it is necessary to modify the structured experience to fit the unique needs and priorities of the particular cultural context of the learner. Each structured exercise focuses on a different aspect of the cultural context to demonstrate the complexity imposed by cultural differences on accuracy in decisional interviewing.

Think of the structured exercise activities as a safe context in which the decisional interviewer can feel free to take risks. The structured

1.1
The Label Exercise

Objective
To show how we often attach labels to people, behave toward them accordingly, and thereby limit our perceptions and restrict communication in our interviews. The exercises should increase the interviewer's awareness of culturally defined labels for the interviewer as well as the client.

Procedure
Class members choose a variety of labels to categorize people. Some samples are as follows: Tell me I'm right. Flatter me. Ignore me. Criticize me. Treat me as a sex object or tell me I'm sexy. Interrupt me. Tell me I'm wrong. Treat me as a helpless person with nothing worthwhile to say.

A less risky but almost as effective alternative is to generate a list of labels so that each label identifies a *positive adjective* such as FRIENDLY, HELPFUL, SEXY, GENEROUS, LOVING.

The labels should be typed or printed on self-adhesive stickers (e.g., Avery index stickers), with enough stickers for all participants.

The instructor divides participants into groups of 6. The groups engage in discussion on a topic for 10 minutes, after which there is a large group discussion on the topic. During the discussion, each member has a "label" on his/her forehead for other members to follow. Each member in the small group gets a different label. No one should know what is on his or her own head. All participants should treat the others in the group as though the labels were true. If it would be culturally insensitive to put the label on the forehead, use the person's back where the wearer cannot see his or her own label.

At the end of 10 minutes, each participant is to guess what his or her label says. Each member is to convey to the group how he or she felt about how the others were acting toward them. After impressions are checked out and confirmed, the person may peel off the label and see what it says. When all members have had a chance to see their label, they return to a large group for discussion. See how other groups experienced the exercise. How might this situation apply to situations one experiences in real life? Identify words used, nonverbal behaviors, and emotional reactions.

Insight   All of us are treated by others according to labels they attach to us.

1.2
Stereotypes of Different Groups

Objective   The interviewer needs to be aware of stereotypes by oneself as interviewer as well as by the client. Without this awareness, the stereotypes will become more important than the real live client actually being interviewed.

Procedure   1. List five different cultures within your discussion group and rank order them in conjunction with the statements below. Add up the total score for each statement on each ethnic group.

2. Address your rankings with at least the following questions:

3. Discuss the following questions:

Why does stereotyping persist?

Is it useful?

Harmful?

What kind of situations tend to stereotype people?

Are positive stereotypes as bad as negative stereotypes?

If several persons undertook this exercise, what similarities in ratings exist? Were there few or different answers to each item? Are there any sex and age differences noted in the ratings?

Groups | A B C D E | Statements |
| --- | --- |
| | Not at all aggressive |
| | Conceited about appearance |
| | Very ambitious |

A B C D E	*Statements*
	Almost always acts as a leader
	Does not hide emotions at all, very independent
	Sneaky
	Cries easily
	Very active
	Very logical
	Not at all competitive
	Feelings easily hurt
	Not at all emotional
	Very strong need for security
	Easily influenced
	Very objective
	Has difficulty making decisions
	Dependent
	Likes math and science very much
	Very passive
	Very direct
	Knows the way of the world
	Excitable in a minor crisis
	Very adventurous
	Very submissive
	Hard working
	Industrious
	Not comfortable about being assertive

Discuss the following questions:

What similarities in ratings exist?

Were there few or many different answers to each item?

Are there any sex and age differences noted in the ratings?

Why does stereotyping persist?

Is it useful?

Harmful?

What kind of situations tend to stereotype people?

Insight   Stereotypes control our thinking with or without our permission.

□

1.3
Stereotypes
as Beliefs

Objective   All interviews are influenced by stereotypes, and interviewers need to define stereotypes and to become more aware of where we find stereotypes and how they are reinforced (e.g., by the media). Stereotypes are defined by generalizations based on some fact, attributes, or categories and label.

Procedure   1.   Ask the group to complete the following statements on a separate sheet of paper. Group members can answer according to their own personal opinions or according to what they think "everybody knows" about the particular groups mentioned.

       a.   "Almost everyone would agree that intelligent, educated, assertive American women today are _____."

       b.   "Some consistent, personal characteristics of people over the age of 65 are _____."

       c.   "It is common knowledge that Blacks raised in the ghetto are _____."

       d.   "Some of the problems with Asian Americans are _____."

       e.   (True or False) "Almost everyone belonging to a minority group would agree that most middle-class Whites are racist."

    2.   Have each group member complete statements and hand papers in to facilitator.

    3.   Have several volunteers read the answers to each question while group monitors make observations of the answers. Also have one volunteer for each question take notes on the answers and be ready to facilitate a discussion later.

    4.   Discuss each statement for about 15 minutes, beginning with the volunteer who took notes. Focusing on key words in each statement

and on questions dealing with where we got the answers, how does the media influence the development and maintenance of stereotypes?

a. Assertive women are often confused with being masculine, aggressive, and "women libbers."

b. Just what do we mean by consistent, personal characteristics? Do old people begin to act in certain manners because we expect them to?

c. How many people are familiar enough with a Black ghetto to have an idea of what life is like there? Where does the word "ghetto" come from? What do we mean by ghetto? How does the media influence our "expectations" that Blacks and ghettos go hand in hand?

d. How do we define Asian Americans? Really, what are some of the problems that Asians themselves identify as being part of a minority in the United States? Who has the problem?

e. What is a middle-class White? How do we define the word racist?

Insight   There is more than one legitimate approach to education across cultures.

1.4
World Picture Test

Objective
Content-based interviews on international topics need to clarify participants' understanding of countries and cultures of the world through their knowledge of geography. The participants will increase in their awareness of the proportionate size and shape of different countries that will help them in interviewing persons from those countries and cultural contexts.

Procedure
1. Give each participant a sheet of paper and a pen and ask all to
   a. draw a map of the world as best they can within a 5-minute time period;
   b. name as many of the countries as they can;
   c. check mark any country they have visited for a week or longer;
   d. exchange papers with other members of the group, and discuss what differences are evidenced in what the other person put into their drawing and/or left out of the drawing.
2. Discuss the following points:
   a. Does a person's awareness of the shape of a country reveal that person's awareness of the shape of the culture?
   b. When a person leaves out a country, what does this mean?
   c. When a person leaves out a continent, what does this mean?
   d. What country did the person place in the center of the map, and what does that mean?
   e. When a person draws a country out of place in relation to other countries, what does this mean?
   f. Were they better acquainted with countries they had visited?
   g. When a person objects violently to doing the drawing, what does that mean?

h. How well did persons draw home countries of other group members?

i. What do the persons plan to do as a result of what they learned in this exercise?

Insight   The more familiar you are with a country, the more accurate you are likely to be in your picture of that country.

1.5 The Cultural Perspectives of Education in Society

Objective

Polemical or argumentative interviews in educational settings depend on an awareness of how divergent and alternative perspectives for viewing education highlight differences in educational values in a multicultural educational environment. Participants will become more aware of how apparently conflicting perspectives of education might each be reasonable in their own context.

Procedure

Read the following directions to a group. "In multicultural education generally, it seems to me that we teacher-learners are in the middle of an argument. Our problem is to restate the argument in such a way that we can settle it. What we are ready for is to try to understand what we know about learning wherever it occurs and to see what the implications are for classroom situations. The most simple expression of the argument is through a sampling of the value conflicts it contains in two cultural perspectives."

Perspective A

"I want my child to be treated as an *individual* by teachers who *center* their attention on the *children* and see themselves essentially as *guides*. Children are capable of *planning* and *discussing* their experiences, of being *guided from within*. The important thing is understanding and *insight* that leads to *growth*. I want them through firsthand experience to learn the meaning of *freedom*, to understand and be committed to a *democratic* way of life. But, above all, I want them to be adequate people, with a rich and ennobling *subjective inner life*; only thus can they achieve the creative *spontaneity* which is man's most precious attribute."

Perspective B   "The teachers are instruments of *society* and are hired primarily because of their mastery in the sciences and the arts as arranged in *school subjects*. Their job is to give *instruction* and to communicate not single interesting facts but rather ideas organized in meaningful relationship to each other, as in a *lecture*. Teachers know the material to be covered, and it is their responsibility *to plan* in such a way that it will be covered. Teachers know that getting ahead in this world requires ability to meet the *demands of the community,* and that only through *drill and practice* can school *achievement* become part of one's habit pattern. Many of the important things in life were discovered by others and are learned through *vicarious experience dominated* by these great *authorities*. The child is free to think as he wishes, but in the objective world of action he or she must *conform* to the standard of the community that describes your own commitment to basic aims of education in society.

Circle the number in the following semantic differential:

Individual	1	2	3	4	5	6	7	Society
Child-centered	1	2	3	4	5	6	7	Subject-centered
Guidance	1	2	3	4	5	6	7	Instruction
Discussion	1	2	3	4	5	6	7	Lecture
Pupil planning	1	2	3	4	5	6	7	Teacher planning
Intrinsic motivation	1	2	3	4	5	6	7	Extrinsic motivation
Insight learning	1	2	3	4	5	6	7	Drill and practice
Growth	1	2	3	4	5	6	7	Achievement
Firsthand experience	1	2	3	4	5	6	7	Vicarious experience
Freedom	1	2	3	4	5	6	7	Dominance
Democratic	1	2	3	4	5	6	7	Authoritarian
Subjective world	1	2	3	4	5	6	7	Objective world
Spontaneity	1	2	3	4	5	6	7	Conformity

Insight   There is more than one way to look at the ideal educational process.

Thelen, H. A. (1956). *Dynamics of Groups at Work*. Chicago: University of Chicago. Adapted and modified by permission.

1.6
A Free Drawing Test

Objective   The interviewing agenda depends on data from differential subconscious responses to culture-loaded concepts that can be discovered via a free drawing test. Participants will increase their own self-awareness of how they might otherwise impose their own agenda on a client during the interview.

Procedure   1. Select a number of concepts (nouns, verbs, etc.) that seem to the group members to be clearly related to their respective cultures.

2. Ask each member to draw an "X" in the middle of a blank sheet of paper.

3. Ask each member to place his or her pencil on the center of the "X" and begin drawing when the facilitator mentions one of the previously selected concepts. The members should not be given any guidance on what to draw but merely instructed to form one continuous line in any direction or shape as they are motivated by the announced concept.

4. Apply a scoring technique to compare the drawings, looking at the data according to whether the drawing is open, closed, large, small, complex, simple, requiring more time, requiring less time, angular, rounded, number of directional changes, number of reversals, recognizable picture, begins with an upstroke, begins with a downstroke, ends with an upstroke, ends with a downstroke, and so forth. Other criteria to compare the drawings may be suggested by the group, growing out of apparent similarities and differences.

5. Discuss whether similarities and differences in the drawings seem to coincide with cultural differences in the group in terms of the covert effects that culture has on behavior.

Insight   Not all our culturally learned patterns are completely conscious.

1.7
Cultural Impact Storytelling

Objective
A credible interviewer may need to stimulate new perceptions and development of new knowledge through storytelling. The American Indians, along with many other ethnic groups, use storytelling as a major vehicle in disseminating their culture. Such an activity is what stimulated Alex Haley to trace his "roots." Many cultures fell away from the art of storytelling with the advent of mass-production printed communication. Storytelling, however, assists us to quite vividly get in touch with our personal "histories" and thus to know more of ourselves (Freire, 1993). By recounting the events, the joys, the sorrows, the people, and the decisions that make us uniquely ourselves, we may realize perceptions and knowledge of how we have been impacted culturally. Participants will become more aware of the stories that define their own cultural context.

Procedure
As you perform the exercise, think specifically of those people or events that, from a cultural perspective, significantly affected you.

1. Using large sheets of paper and crayons, graphically (i.e. using symbols, sketches, etc.) represent the events, the joys, the sorrows, the people, and the decisions that have had an effect on your unique cultural development.

2. Now, looking over your story, place a plus (+) sign by one event you consider a highly positive experience. Next, place a negative (–) sign by one event you consider an extremely negative experience.

3. Before your group, "tell your story." First, hang the graphic where all can see. As you come to them, describe in detail your "+" and "–" experiences.

4. Analyze variables that were operative, thus creating either a positive or a negative impact. In attempting to understand the dynamics of the two variables, can the variables be explained with a concept or a theory?

Insight   Much of our thinking process is guided by culturally learned stories.

1.8
Cultural Bias

Objective   A good interviewer needs to become more aware of other ways to approach a situation. One important barrier to cross-cultural communication is your own cultural bias. If we are limited to understanding all other people from our own cultural point of view, then we are trapped by a limited and rigid set of rules. Participants will become more aware of their own self-reference criterion as it distorts their perspective of a client's cultural context.

Procedure   Copies of the following list are handed out to members of the group. Each participant is to circle five adjectives describing people they like and underline five adjectives describing people they do not like to be around. Participants may add adjectives of their own. Wherever possible, the adjectives should be related to specific cultural groups.

adventurous	good listener	shy
affectionate	helpful	soft on subordinates
ambitious	independent	stern
appreciative	indifferent to others	submissive
argumentative	intolerant	successful
competitive	jealous	sympathetic
complaining	kind	tactful
considerate of others	loud	talkative
discourteous	neat	teasing
distant	needs much praise	thorough
dominating	obedient	thoughtful
easily angered	optimistic	touchy, cannot be kidded
easily discouraged	orderly	trusting
easily influenced	rebellious	uncommunicative
efficient	responsible	understanding
enthusiastic	sarcastic	varied interests
false	self-centered	very dependent on others
forgiving	self-respecting	warm
fun-loving	self-satisfied	well-mannered
gives praise readily	shrewd, devious	willing worker

Insight   We each have our own cultural biases.

Adapted from Anne Pedersen, *Cross-Cultural Concepts,* unpublished manuscript.

1.9
Dialogue
Within Ourselves

Objective   An intentional interviewer needs help to gain practice in listening to and making cultural interpretations of "internal dialogue" about others on a given cross-cultural issue that generates ambivalent thoughts and feelings. Participants will become more aware of how their own culturally learned assumptions express themselves in the decisional interview.

Procedure   1.   Select a cross-cultural subject which produces ambivalent thoughts and feelings within you.

2.   Tune in on your ambivalent thoughts, and listen to the two sides of your internal dialogue.

3.   Write down as a script of a play or conversation the dialogue between your internal voices, attempting to identify the emergence of cultural bias.

Insight   Our internal dialogue is often a discussion between positive and negative voices.

1.10
Talking About Multiculturalism in Primary Grades

Objective

An effective interview will deal with differences in a neutral framework without prematurely evaluating those differences in terms of good or bad criteria. We belong to many groups that function in ways similar to cultures and define our individuality in multicultural terms. This exercise was originally used to show primary school children the many groups to which they belong beyond the national or ethnic differences that define them as individuals. Not all decisional interviews will be exclusively with adults, as in cases where the family is involved. This exercise can be modified for adults but has primarily been used in working with children to increase their awareness of similarities and differences in the cultural context.

Procedure

This exercise works well with a moderate to large group of multiethnic primary or intermediate schoolchildren. Their instructors or other school personnel should be present to conduct the exercise and to help interpret its meaning. An average-size school classroom provides sufficient room to accommodate the exercise. Tables and chairs should be moved to one side or to a corner of the room. The exercise may be somewhat noisy. The exercise requires at least 20 minutes to a half hour and should follow a lecture or class discussion about prejudice, discrimination, or problems that persons from some cultures have experienced as a result of being different.

A list of neutral characteristics that would be likely to divide the group should be drawn up beforehand in a series of sets. They may include characteristics such as black shoes/brown shoes/other colored shoes, those wearing red/those not wearing red, those with a penny/those without a penny, and other similarly neutral categories.

1. Students should assemble in a large group in the center of the floor.

2. An instructor reads directions such as "All those wearing red move to the right side of the room, and all those not wearing red move to the left side of the room." The "team" that assembles first "wins" that set. Then, the group reassembles in the center of the floor. Subsequent sets begin with the instructor reading off directions that will divide the group in different ways.

3. After the group has become familiar with the exercise, other differences that are more personal may be used, such as hair color, eye color, tall/short, or other characteristics of the individuals.

4. The more obviously cultural differences such as sex, national background, race, and so forth should be saved for the end.

5. A discussion could center around racial/cultural differences being just one of the significant components of our individuality that define us but should not be used to evaluate our worth. The discussion might focus on the role of competition both in the exercise, where the students were on different teams for each set, and in real life, where persons who are different struggle against one another. The students might be encouraged to share incidents of how they have experienced "differentness" in themselves and in others.

Insight   The shifting dynamics of "salience similarity" cross over differences across cultures.

PART

II

Structured
Exercises and
Experiences
to Increase
Knowledge

The second set of exercises focuses on increasing the interviewer's knowledge or comprehension of what a client's cultural context "means." The exercises will protect the interviewer from being misled by his or her own self-reference criterion, which imposes the interviewer's perspective on each client. The interviewer will be better able to differentiate both similarities and differences across cultural contexts through these exercises. These exercises will prepare the interviewer to comprehend the client's cultural context in its own terms.

2.1
Interviewing Local Resource Persons

Objective

To show the importance of including resource persons from the host culture in training visitors. Resource persons know much about their home culture that is not published in written materials, but it is sometimes difficult for them to respond if asked to "tell about" their own culture. By working with these resource persons, the interviewer will increase his or her knowledge of the interviewing context.

Procedure

Three exercises are provided to access the resource person's expertise in training situations.

1. A resource person describes a local situation that required a difficult decision, briefing the group for about 5 minutes on the background for making a decision but *not revealing to the group what decision was actually made.*

   Then, each member of the group should say what he or she thought the resource person decided to do and why. After each group member has had a chance to guess, the resource person will say what was actually decided and why.

2. Each person in the group makes one statement about the culture represented by the resource person based on the group member's previous experience and then asks the resource person a question about the local culture. After all the members of the group have had a chance to reveal their own experiences with the local culture and ask a question, the resource person describes the attitudes of the group and what the members could do to increase their accuracy of intercultural perception.

3. A resource person stands in front of the group and carries on a conversation with one of the group members. Another person is assigned to stand behind each of the speakers and say aloud what he or she thinks the person is thinking but not saying as the two people carry out their conversation.

    The observing classroom group then has a picture of both the spoken and unspoken levels of communication in the exchange. The exchange and side comments may be videotaped and the videotape played back to the class later for analysis and discussion.

Insight   Not all cultural similarities and differences are obvious.

2.2
A Personal
Cultural History

Objective   A background interview will help the interviewer become more knowledgeable of how each cultural context controls our lives by systematically describing our own personal cultural history.

Procedure   Complete the following questionnaire:

1. Describe the earliest memory you have of an experience with a person (people) of a cultural or ethnic group different from your own.

2. Who or what has had the most influence in the formation of your attitudes and opinions about people of different cultural groups? In what way?

3. What influences in your experiences have led to the development of positive feelings about your own cultural heritage and background?

4. What influences in your experiences have led to the development of negative feelings, if any, about your own cultural heritage or background?

5. What changes if any, would you like to make in your own attitudes or experiences in relation to people of other ethnic or cultural groups?

6. Describe an experience in your own life when you feel you were discriminated against for any reason, not necessarily because of your culture.

7. How do you feel people should deal with (or not deal with) issues of cultural diversity in American society?

Discuss the similarities and differences of group member responses to the same questions.

Insight   Each of us has a culture.

2.3
No Questions Asked

Objective   Good interviewers can perceive the other person's viewpoint by comprehending the context in its own terms as offering clues to the nature of the cultural community context in which they find themselves. Participants will increase their knowledge of the cultural context for interviewing.

Procedure   As this exercise is designed to be "free-form" and thereby difficult to control, it requires that the facilitator have a good knowledge of the cultural community and be alert to any errors in observation.

1. Send participants into the community for at least one afternoon with instructions to learn as much about it as possible without asking direct questions—preferably without asking questions at all.
2. In group discussions, the facilitator is to ask specific questions about the community.

Insight   Much can be learned without asking questions by watching and listening in another culture.

Developed by Paul B. Pedersen, Syracuse University.

2.4
Role-Playing a Newspaper Incident

Objective   Good interviewers learn perspective taking by demonstrating how persons from different backgrounds see everyday events differently that involve persons from more than one culture. Participants will increase their knowledge and comprehension of each newspaper article from a variety of different viewpoints.

Procedure   1. The facilitator brings one or more newspapers into the group and ask the members to examine the papers.

2. Group members each select from the paper a story involving Asian Americans with which they can identify and which could possibly have happened to them personally.

3. Each member of the group must project him- or herself into the role of one main person in the selected story and tell the group about what happened as though it had happened to him or her personally. Group members are free to ask questions of each person telling the story to explicate aspects of the story that they find difficult to understand.

Insight   Learning about multiculturalism causes you to read the newspapers with greater insight.

Developed by Paul Pedersen, Syracuse University.

2.5
Cross-Cultural Training Exercise for Interpreting Policy

Objective   Administrative interviews depend on culture-specific patterns of common and variant interpretations as well as a level of comprehension of written material containing word deletions. Participants will increase their knowledge about different policies as they impose their own organizational constraints on both the client and the interviewer.

Procedure   1.   The facilitator selects one or more paragraphs drawn from institutional rhetoric involving cross-cultural values.
2.   The facilitator then omits at least 10 or 15 words, keeping the space where these words were extracted blank for the participants to write in their own words they consider appropriate.
3.   Each participant is given a copy of the paragraph and a pencil.
4.   Then, after filling in the blanks to give the paragraph meaning, the participants compare their interpretations and discuss them according to culture-specific variables.

Insight   Institutional policy contains many implicit cultural assumptions.

2.6
Cultural Value Systems
With Conflicting
Points of View

Objective   Good mediating interviews will demonstrate contrasting and conflicting aspects of interactions between persons who do not share the
same basic assumptions by discussing value conflicts. Participants will
become more knowledgeable about how each cultural context contains
conflicting viewpoints.

Procedure   1. Divide into two or more individual or group units.

2. Generate alternative value systems from the members' own backgrounds (example: a system that is property or rule oriented and one
that is person oriented).

3. Assign each value system to one of the individual or group units.

4. Discuss a topic in which those value systems are likely to be contrasting or conflicting with one another.

5. Require each individual or group unit to maintain a position consistent with the assigned value system.

6. Assign one or more observers to take votes and referee.

7. Evaluate each group according to the criteria of:

    a. whether they maintained a position consistent with their as-
    signed value system,

    b. whether they were more skillful in developing a powerful argu-
    ment for their position based on these borrowed values.

Insight   Cultures are not always in agreement on important issues.

Developed by Paul Pedersen, Syracuse University.

2.7
Michigan International Student Problem Inventory

Objective

Clinical interviewers of internationals may need to define problems or areas of conflict that an international student may be experiencing. Participants will increase their knowledge about the problems and issues confronting the international students.

Procedure

Read the following directions to a group of international students: "You are not being tested. There are no right or wrong answers. This is a list of statements about situations that occasionally trouble (perturb, distress, annoy, grieve, or worry) students from other countries who are attending college in the United States. The statements are related to area of admissions, academic work, language, religion, and so forth."

PLEASE FOLLOW THESE STEPS:

Step 1—Read the list of statements carefully, pause at each statement, and if it suggests a situation that is troubling you, circle the number to the left of the statement.

Step 2—After completing Step 1, go back over the numbers you have circled, and place an X in the circle of the statements that are of most concern to you.

1. Evaluation of my former school
2. Concern about value of U.S. credentials education
3. Choosing college subjects
4. Treatment received at orientation meetings
5. Unfavorable remarks about home country
6. Concept of being a "foreign" student
7. Frequent college examinations
8. Compulsory class attendance
9. Writing or typing term (semester) papers
10. Concern about becoming too "Westernized"
11. Insufficient personal-social counseling
12. Being in love with someone
13. Taste of food in United States
14. Problems regarding housing
15. Being told where one must live
16. Poor eye sight
17. Recurrent headaches
18. My physical height and physique
19. Religious practice in the United States
20. Attending church socials
21. Concern about my religious beliefs
22. Speaking English
23. Giving oral reports in class
24. Ability to write English
25. Regulations on student activities
26. Treatment received at social events
27. Relationship of men and women in the United States
28. Lack of money to meet expenses
29. Not receiving enough money from home
30. Having to do manual labor (with hands)
31. Finding a job upon returning home
32. Not enough time in United States for study
33. Trying to extend stay in the United States
34. Getting admitted to a U.S. college
35. Registration for classes each term
36. Not attending college of my first choice
37. Relationship with foreign students
38. Leisure time activities of U.S. advisor students
39. Law enforcement practices in the United States
40. Competitive college grading system

41. Objective examinations (true-false, etc.)
42. Insufficient advice from academic advisor
43. Being lonely
44. Feeling inferior to others
45. Trying to make friends
46. Costs of buying food
47. Insufficient clothing
48. Not being able to room with U.S. student
49. Hard to hear
50. Nervousness
51. Finding adequate health services
52. Finding worship group of own faith
53. Christianity as a philosophy
54. Variety of religious faith in the United States
55. Reciting in class
56. Understanding lectures in English
57. Reading textbooks written in English
58. Dating practices of U.S. people
59. Being accepted in social groups
60. Not being able to find "dates"
61. Saving enough money for social events
62. Immigration work restrictions
63. Limited amount U.S. dollar will purchase
64. Becoming a citizen of the United States
65. Changes in home government
66. Desire to not return to home country
67. Understanding college catalogs
68. Immigration regulations
69. Lack of knowledge about the United States
70. Campus size
71. U.S. emphasis on time and promptness
72. Understanding how to use the library
73. Too many interferences with studies
74. Feel unprepared for U.S. college work
75. Concerned about grades
76. Sexual customs in the United States
77. Homesickness
78. Feeling superior to others
79. Bathroom facilities cause problems
80. Distances to classes from residence

81. Relationship with roommate
82. Dietary problems
83. Need more time to rest
84. Worried about mental health
85. Having time to devote to own religion
86. Spiritual versus materialistic values
87. Doubting the value of any religion
88. Understanding U.S. slang
89. My limited English vocabulary
90. My pronunciation not understood
91. Activities of International Houses
92. U.S. emphasis on sports
93. Problems when shopping in the United States
94. Finding part-time work
95. Unexpected financial needs
96. Money for clothing
97. Uncertainties in the world today
98. Desire to enroll at another college
99. U.S. education not what was expected
100. Differences in purposes among U.S. educational institutions
101. Differences in U.S. and home education
102. Not being met on arrival at campus
103. College orientation program sufficient
104. Trying to be student and tourist
105. Attitude of some students to foreigners
106. Doing laboratory assignments
107. Insufficient personal help from U.S. professors
108. Relationship between students and faculty
109. U.S. emphasis on personal habits of cleanliness
110. Not feeling at ease in public
111. Attitude of some U.S. people to skin color
112. Finding a place to live between college terms
113. Changes in weather conditions
114. Lack of invitations
115. Feeling under tension
116. Service received at health center
117. Health suffering due to academic pace
118. Criticisms of homeland religion
119. Accepting differences in great religions
120. Confusion about religion and morals in the United States

121. Insufficient remedial English services
122. Having a non-English-speaking roommate
123. Holding a conversation with U.S. friend
124. Activities of foreign student organization
125. Lack of opportunities to meet more people
126. Concern about political U.S. "ambassador" discussions
127. Costs of an automobile
128. Finding employment between college terms
129. Finding jobs that will pay well
130. Insufficient help from placement office
131. Staying in the United States and getting a job
132. Wonder if U.S. education is useful for job at home

Insight   Some problems occur to international students with greater frequency than others.

Porter, J. W., & Haller, A. D. (1962). *Michigan International Student Problem Inventory*. East Lansing, MI: International Programs, Michigan State University. Adapted by permission.

2.8
A Simulation Designing Exercise "Multipoly"

Objective

A technique of group interviewing is to identify the significant aspects of an intercultural situation or event on a game board and simulate intercultural interaction with a small group working together to design and play the simulation. Participants will increase their knowledge about specific and contrasting aspects within and between cultural contexts as they might influence decisional interviewing.

Procedure

The process you are about to begin is quite serious and will demand considerable investment of time and energy but will, we hope, result in a product both stimulating and useful in your group and/or organization.

Take the rules for a well-known board game from the following pages and rewrite those rules to fit the conditions of six different ethnic, racial, or cultural roles. The "rules" for each role will differ in this game as they do in real life. You will be sensitive to the different advantages and disadvantages facing each role; to the different aspirations and goals to which each role aspires; to the different acceptable and unacceptable ways of doing things for each role; and to the different "style" that applies not only to each role group as perceived by themselves but also as perceived by outsiders. You will ask yourself, for example:

- "Does each of the six groups have the same ultimate goal? Money? Influence? Popularity? Power?"
- "Does each group begin the game with the same resources in terms of money, power, or opportunity?"

When the project is complete, there will be *six different sets of rules* for the game and all will be able to attempt to play the same game together *simultaneously,* each of the six players being guided by a different set of rules.

Change the name of the game to Multipoly or some other more appropriate (and not registered) title as, for example, "Multiculturalism." You will be responsible for drawing up different sets of rules independently and then dividing into groups of six persons, one for each role, to coordinate your ideas into one set of rules for that role.

You will also want to indigenize the place names on the game board and develop new sets of "chance"- and "community chest"-type cards to fit the situation you are simulating. The steps for designing the game are as follows:

1. Identify policy objectives for each culture being represented.
2. Identify intercultural situations where the participating cultures are likely to interact for each space around the edge of the game board.
3. Identify the problems each situation would create for each participating culture and assign a negative score to the space.
4. Identify the opportunities each situation would create for each participating culture and assign a positive score to the space.
5. Assign a net positive or a net negative score and consequence for each participating culture relative to each situation.
6. Identify additional solutions through the "chance"- or "community chest"-type decks of cards available to players landing on designated spaces.
7. Design each participating culture role to accurately reflect the balance of feasibility and cost-benefit testing of alternative choices interacting with the other cultures in society.
8. Design the game so that a player in one culture role will finish the game knowing more of that culture's role in society than previously.
9. Design the game so that a player in one culture role will see the advantages and disadvantages of meeting the needs of other cultures outside the person's own group through cooperation.
10. Provide opportunities for discussion of how the system could be changed toward a more equitable distribution of opportunities across racial and cultural Multipoly.

(You fill in the situations for the game board)

Insight   There will be advantages and disadvantages for each cultural group in a cooperative/competitive relationship with other cultures.

2.9
Partners:
a Sex-Role
Training Exercise

Objective

Interviewers across genders may need to train themselves and a partner of the opposite sex in awareness of sex-role stereotyped perceptions of one another. Participants will increase their knowledge about the opposite gender in general and a particular person from that opposite gender in particular.

Instructions

Sex roles resemble cultures as they shape individual values, perceptions, and decisions. To complete this exercise, a larger group of colleagues would be divided into partners so that one partner would be a male and the other a female. Each partner would respond to the 47 questions or tasks in the exercise and then exchange responses to discuss their perceptions with one another. After all partner teams have completed their responses and discussed their perceptions, the total group can be assembled to discuss the effect of sex-role stereotyping in their particular organization or group.

Sex-role stereotyping has become a topic of controversy, giving rise to accusations, counteraccusations, anger, and victimization of both male and female colleagues. This training program attempts to reduce the conflict between different-sex colleagues in several ways:

1. The exercise will relate to factual, data-based research conclusions about sex-role stereotyping rather than emotional accusations or unfounded generalities.

2. The exercise will be limited to the private and confidential exchange between two different-sex colleagues without involving other outsiders.

3. The exercise requires the two participant colleagues, one male and one female, to apply the research findings to their own and their partner's situation, thereby personalizing the otherwise abstract research conclusions.

The objectives of this exercise are to facilitate a private, nonformal educational exchange between a male and a female colleague on sex-role stereotypes in career development. The two participants will have selected one another in a contract to complete the program, exchange information about themselves and how they perceive their partner, discussing what they have learned with one another.

The optimum outcome of participation in this exercise will be to

1. increase the participant's motivation for a more comprehensive training program in sex-role stereotypes

2. exchange perceptions with a different sex colleague on how each partner sees themselves in relation to the other

3. strengthen the collegial relationship with a colleague from the opposite sex on issues of sex-role stereotyping

The research on which this exercise is based was collected through the project Born Free and is cited in *Selected Review of the Literature on Career Development and Sex-Role Stereotyping at the Post/Secondary/Higher Educational Level,* Born Free, Technical Report No. 3, Department of Psycho-educational Studies, University of Minnesota, Minneapolis, August 1977.

Each capitalized statement describes a research finding conclusion. You will be directed to apply each statement to yourself and/or your partner. Please write your response on the same page as the statement and question. After writing in a response to each of the items, exchange booklets with your partner and discuss your responses. DO NOT DISCUSS YOUR RESPONSES OR THESE ITEMS WITH YOUR PARTNER UNTIL YOU HAVE BOTH RESPONDED TO EACH ITEM AND EXCHANGED BOOKLETS.

1. Identical products are evaluated more highly when attributed to a male rather than a female.

    1.1 Can you think of an example where you may have evaluated a behavior by one sex differently than the same behavior by someone from the opposite sex?

1.2 Can you think of an example where your partner may have evaluated a behavior by one sex differently than the same behavior by someone from the opposite sex?

2. As they grow up, women are taught to value men more and value themselves less.

    2.1 Can you recall a statement from your own childhood where boys were described as superior to girls by a respected adult?

    2.2 Would you expect your partner to teach his/her children that boys are superior to girls even though he/she may not be aware of having taught that lesson?

3. Women have greater verbal ability than men, while men excel in visual-spacial ability, mathematical ability, and tend to be more aggressive.

    3.1 What differences did you first become aware of between yourself and persons of the opposite sex?

    3.2 How do you think your partner saw him or herself as different from the opposite sex as a child?

4. Women with a more innovative role or lifestyle tend to have nonstereotypical views of themselves in terms of sex roles.

    4.1 Would you describe yourself and your partner as "innovative" in your lifestyles?

    4.2 Would you describe yourself and your partner as having a stereotypical view of yourselves in terms of sex roles?

5. The learning of adult sex roles is seen primarily as occupation-directed for males and family-directed for females.

    5.1 What did your parents want you to be when you grew up and why?

    5.2 What are some other careers where you think your partner might have enjoyed success?

6. Women with nontraditional attitudes toward their family not only fantasized more achievement but actually achieved higher grades in college.

    6.1 Would you describe the high-achieving women you know as having nontraditional attitudes toward the traditional family?

    6.2 Describe one nontraditional attitude of your partner toward the family.

7. Women who are competent and achieve are viewed as deviant from norms for women and thus anxious, whereas women who see themselves as lacking these traits may suffer low self-esteem.

    7.1 If you were given the choice, would you prefer to be viewed as competent (but deviant) or traditional (but lacking in self-esteem)?

7.2 Are competent and achieving men less anxious than competent and achieving women?

8. Woman have a more difficult time seeking a career congruent with their self-concept than men.

8.1 Is your career congruent with your self-concept?

8.2 Is your partner's career congruent with his/her self-concept?

9. Women who have clearly differentiated concepts of career woman and homemaker are more likely to have work plans congruent with their self-image, whether that is as homemaker or as career woman.

9.1 Do you differentiate between career woman and homemaker roles as two legitimate directions for men *and* women?

9.2 Does your partner differentiate between both roles as legitimate for men *and* women.

10. Men who see themselves as competent have higher self-esteem than men who are not perceived as competent or successful.

10.1 What are the criteria by which you might describe yourself as competent?

10.2 What are the criteria by which you might describe your partner as competent?

11. Men and women do not differ on the locus of control until college when women tend to score higher on measures of external locus of control than men.

11.1 Do you tend to believe that most of your decisions are controlled by others or external sources of power?

11.2 Do you think your partner feels that most decisions are controlled by others or external sources?

12. High school women who scored higher on internal locus of control measures chose more innovative careers than did those with higher external locus of control scores.

12.1 Are you attracted to unusual and innovative career choices?

12.2 Do you think your partner is attracted to unusual and innovative career choices?

13. Sex-role stereotypes of greater male control and power occur even in elementary school textbooks when male characters cause good things to happen by their own actions, whereas female characters profit from the actions of others or from fortuitous circumstances.

13.1 Give an example of a fictional hero/heroine who rescues others that you admired or enjoyed learning about.

13.2 Give an example of a fictional hero/heroine who reminds you of your partner in some way.

14. Persons with higher scores on internal control measures work harder for success.

14.1 Do you consider a high score on internal control measures to be "sex fair" as an evaluation criteria?

14.2 Do you think your partner would describe this measure as sex fair or unbiased?

15. Women who subscribe to system blame aspire to less typical feminine roles and are more likely to seek careers outside the home.

15.1 Do you think it is good and right to blame the system for being sexist?

15.2 Do you think your partner would say it is good and right to blame the system?

16. College students of both sexes who have strong internal control beliefs describe themselves more positively and with more traits seen as stereotypically characteristic of the opposite sex.

16.1 What are some of your personality traits that you would characterize as more typically belonging to the opposite sex?

16.2 What are some of your partner's personality traits that you would characterize as more typically belonging to the opposite sex?

17. Increases in internal control beliefs are reported following participation in a community action program when links between old successes and new goals are explicitly pointed out and when sources of possible reinforcement are described.

17.1 Do you see yourself as tending to see your decisions more and more controlled by internal or by external factors?

17.2 Do you see your partner's decisions as being more and more controlled by internal or by external factors?

18. Women do not achieve as much as men in the professions, politics, and sports according to traditional measures of success.

18.1 In what ways would you consider yourself more "successful" than your partner?

18.2 In what ways would you consider your partner more successful than yourself?

19. Women experience a conflict between success and femininity but do not exhibit a greater "fear of success" than men.

19.1 Can you describe a particular incident where you seemed to avoid success?

19.2 Can you describe a particular incident where your partner seemed to avoid success?

20. Although women have as high an achievement motivation as men, they are more likely to focus their efforts on achievement in traditionally defined feminine tasks just as men are more likely to focus on masculine task roles.

20.1   In what ways do you think you have a higher achievement motivation than your partner?

20.2   In what ways do you think your partner has a higher achievement motivation than yourself?

21.   When a group of males and females are asked to predict how well they will perform on a specified task, women state lower expectations for their performance than men do.

21.1   Describe a particular task that you can do better than your partner.

21.2   Describe a particular task that your partner can do better than yourself.

22.   Women's expectancies of success in various tasks requiring visual spacial or math abilities decline in adolescence.

22.1   How have your visual-spacial or math abilities contributed or not contributed to your success?

22.2   How have your partner's similar abilities contributed or not contributed to success?

23.   Men and women do not differ significantly in the accuracy of their performance estimations but do differ in the direction of error, with males tending to overestimate their performance and women to underestimate theirs.

23.1   Give an example of when you overestimated your performance and an example of when you underestimated your performance.

23.2   Give two similar examples of your partner.

24.   Women may be underrepresented in many prestigious occupations not only because of external barriers that limit access but also because of internal attitudinal barriers that lead women not to aspire to such professions.

24.1   Give an example of an external barrier and an internal barrier that inhibited your career.

24.2   Give an example of an external barrier and an internal barrier that you think inhibited your partner's career.

25.   Compared to females, males have higher career aspirations and anticipate more successful performance in a variety of tasks.

25.1   Do you have career aspirations that are higher than your partner's?

25.2   Does your partner have higher career aspirations than you do?

26.   Men and women tend to have different patterns of attribution to explain the outcomes of their performance, with women tending to attribute unexpected success to luck and expected failure to lack of ability.

26.1   Describe a recent success of your own explaining why it was successful.

26.2   Describe a recent success of your partner explaining why it was successful.

27.   Women tend to attribute both success and failure to external causes such as task difficulty or luck so that they feel less pride in success and less shame at failure than males do.

27.1   Describe a recent failure of your own, explaining why it was a failure.

27.2   Describe a recent failure of your partner, explaining why it was a failure.

28.   There is sex discrimination in the awarding of financial assistance for college students so that women get less than their share of available money.

28.1   How much scholarship assistance did you get toward the completion of your post-high-school education?

28.2   How much scholarship assistance would you estimate your partner received?

29.   Fields are viewed as being masculine or feminine, with more women in professions stereotyped as feminine and more men in professions stereotyped as masculine.

29.1   List the names of at least six persons, known to you and to your partner personally, who are in careers that would traditionally be characterized as more appropriate for the opposite sex.

29.2   Have you ever considered a career that might seem more appropriate for someone from the opposite sex?

30.   Over the past decade, the proportion of first-year college women planning to enter male fields such as business, medicine, law, and engineering has nearly tripled.

30.1   What are the careers you would like to see your male and female children strive for?

30.2   What are the careers you would expect your partner to want his/her male/female children to strive for?

31.   Counselors of both sexes perceive deviate career goals as less appropriate than conforming goals for their female clients and tend to perceive male or female clients with deviate goals as more in need of further counseling.

31.1   If your son or daughter chose a career that counselors described as deviate, would you encourage your son or daughter to continue?

31.2   If your partner's son or daughter chose a career that counselors described as deviate, would your partner encourage the son or daughter to continue?

32. Traditional counselors impute greater maladjustment to female students than to identically described males.

    32.1 Among the eccentric friends you and your partner may both know, cite one male and one female example indicating which one is the most eccentric.

    32.2 In what ways do you see yourself as more or less adjusted to stress situations than your partner is?

33. Male counselors in training while subscribing to a universal standard for healthy males and adults hold another stereotypical conforming standard for healthy females.

    33.1 Write a brief description of a healthy male and a healthy female.

    33.2 Do you expect your partner's comparison to be similar to yours or dissimilar?

34. In counseling, males are more likely to be rated as having vocational-educational problems, whereas females are more often rated as having emotional-social problems.

    34.1 Describe an educational-vocational problem and an emotional-social problem you have experienced or are experiencing.

    34.2 Describe a problem you think your partner might be facing.

35. Counselors are less well informed to counsel women, especially innovative women, than they are to counsel men.

    35.1 Describe the characteristics of a counselor you would seek out for help on your own problems.

    35.2 Describe the characteristics of a counselor that you think your partner would seek out.

36. Career interest measurement inventories contain a sex bias in their use of language.

    36.1 Give some examples of how career interest inventories might contain a sex bias in the use of language.

    36.2 Would you expect your partner to disregard advice from career interest measurement inventories if it ran counter to his/her preferred career?

37. Textbooks frequently portray women in a negatively biased stereotyped manner.

    37.1 Why do you think this might be true?

    37.2 Why do you think your partner will say it might be true?

38. It has been harder for a woman to get admitted to an undergraduate college than for a man.

    38.1 Do you believe a more "qualified" male should be rejected in preference for a less "qualified" female college applicant, or should sex role be disregarded in the question of admissions?

38.2 What do you expect your partner to respond to that question?

39. The majority of professional women (70%) are concentrated in a few professions traditionally considered feminine, such as teaching, nursing, library science, secretarial, and social work.

    39.1 Do you expect future men and women to move into professional roles reserved for the opposite sex in the past?

    39.2 Do you think your partner expects future men and women to move into one another's professional roles?

40. In 1970, nearly half of all women were working because of financial necessity rather than for pleasure or self-fulfillment.

    40.1 What would happen if you were to quit your job?

    40.2 What would happen if your partner quit his/her job?

41. Occupations stereotypically associated with high levels of competence, rationality, and assertion were viewed as masculine, whereas occupations stereotypically viewed as feminine were associated with dependency, passivity, nurturance, and interpersonal warmth.

    41.1 Describe some masculine and feminine characteristics required for your job.

    41.2 Describe some masculine and feminine characteristics required for your partner's job.

42. Although more women are working today than were before, they are not aspiring to positions as high-level as women did 30 years ago.

    42.1 Would you describe yourself as aspiring to a higher-level position than your parents achieved?

    42.2 Would you describe your partner as aspiring to a higher-level position than his/her parents achieved?

43. Role models, especially the maternal model, are closely related to the occupational choices of women and their motivation to pursue these choices.

    43.1 Describe how your parents influenced your choice of career.

    43.2 From knowing your partner's attitudes, describe what you imagine his/her parents' abilities might have been.

44. Women preparing for nontraditional, male-dominated fields (math and science) think men make little differentiation in male-female work roles and other related behaviors or attitudes.

    44.1 Do the male colleagues in your workplace differentiate between male and female work roles?

    44.2 Do you think your partner will say that male colleagues differentiate between male and female work roles?

45. Sex-role perceptions are affected by parental role behaviors, with maternal employment outside the home resulting in smaller perceived sex-role differences.

45.1 How were you influenced by your mother working/not working outside the home?

45.2 Do you believe your partner's mother worked outside the home?

46. In research on sex-role stereotypes, males are described by traits called "competency" attributes, such as being independent, objective, competitive, self-confident, and logical, whereas women are seen as lacking these competency traits and possessing traits of "warmth and expressiveness," such as being gentle, tactful, sensitive to the feelings of others, quiet, and tender. Neither men nor women were typically seen as possessing the traits characteristic of the opposite sex.

46.1 Which traits of the opposite sex do you admire most?

46.2 Which traits of the opposite sex do you think your partner will claim to admire most?

47. Generalized self-esteem measures are as high for women as for men.

47.1 What could you accomplish that would increase your self-esteem?

47.2 What could your partner accomplish that would increase his/her self-esteem?

Insight   Gender roles are learned and are important to the individual's cultural identity.

2.10
The I.I.P.*
Questionnaire

Objective

Clinical interviewers need to understand how the same situation may be seen differently before and after training in multicultural counseling. Participants will increase their knowledge about how those with more training and expertise will define differences as pathology, whereas those with less training and expertise will be more likely to define differences as cultural.

Procedure

Students should fill in the following information before completing the questionnaire. A pseudonym or symbol may be used instead of the student's name. The same pseudonym or symbol should be used on the posttest.

Name _____ Institution _____ Date _____

Number of years as a practicing counselor or psychologist (please circle)
    Under 1 year   1-3 years   4-6 years   7-10 years   Over 10 years

Number of courses taken in counseling or related field (please circle)
    1 course   2-5 courses   6-10 courses   Over 10 courses

Main area of professional interest

Please specify (please circle)
    Pretest   Posttest

    For each incident or situation, indicate the degree to which you feel the problem is interpersonal, intercultural, or psychopathological in nature. Use the definitions of these terms as you currently understand them.

---

*I.I.P. = Interpersonal, Intercultural, and Psychopathological

1 = a totally irrelevant issue in respect to this problem

10 = an extremely important issue in respect to this problem

1. A 35-year-old man lives in a crowded neighborhood in downtown Syracuse, yet feels isolated and alone. He feels people are cold and unfriendly.

    Interpersonal: 1 2 3 4 5 6 7 8 9 10

    Intercultural: 1 2 3 4 5 6 7 8 9 10

    Psychopathological: 1 2 3 4 5 6 7 8 9 10

2. A female college student feels that men are only interested in sex and not in getting to know her as an individual. Although she admits to being very flirtatious, she feels angry and degraded when men respond in a sexual way.

    Interpersonal: 1 2 3 4 5 6 7 8 9 10

    Intercultural: 1 2 3 4 5 6 7 8 9 10

    Psychopathological: 1 2 3 4 5 6 7 8 9 10

3. A case worker indicates to a client (male, head of household) that the client will need to do some of the work that will be needed to find him an apartment and a job. The client is angry and resentful as he feels the caseworker should be doing all these things for him.

    Interpersonal: 1 2 3 4 5 6 7 8 9 10

    Intercultural: 1 2 3 4 5 6 7 8 9 10

    Psychopathological: 1 2 3 4 5 6 7 8 9 10

4. A 28-year-old unmarried woman is extremely reluctant to make any decision without the permission of her father and his full support.

    Interpersonal: 1 2 3 4 5 6 7 8 9 10

    Intercultural: 1 2 3 4 5 6 7 8 9 10

    Psychopathological: 1 2 3 4 5 6 7 8 9 10

5. A 23-year-old woman engages in premarital sex for the first time. She subsequently comes to a counselor suffering from guilt and the fear that she will be viewed by her friends and family as promiscuous.

    Interpersonal: 1 2 3 4 5 6 7 8 9 10

    Intercultural: 1 2 3 4 5 6 7 8 9 10

    Psychopathological: 1 2 3 4 5 6 7 8 9 10

6. A Korean woman has a baby who is delivered in a New York Hospital; all aspects of the delivery are normal. The woman soon becomes depressed as well as feeling angry and resentful towards the hospital staff.

    Interpersonal: 1 2 3 4 5 6 7 8 9 10

    Intercultural: 1 2 3 4 5 6 7 8 9 10

    Psychopathological: 1 2 3 4 5 6 7 8 9 10

7. A person is referred for counseling because he keeps losing jobs because of absenteeism and tardiness.

   Interpersonal: 1 2 3 4 5 6 7 8 9 10
   Intercultural: 1 2 3 4 5 6 7 8 9 10
   Psychopathological: 1 2 3 4 5 6 7 8 9 10

8. A person goes to a counselor for help in choosing a career. As the counselor tries to help the client clarify his feelings and attitudes about different careers, the client becomes very angry and frustrated.

   Interpersonal: 1 2 3 4 5 6 7 8 9 10
   Intercultural: 1 2 3 4 5 6 7 8 9 10
   Psychopathological: 1 2 3 4 5 6 7 8 9 10

9. A person is referred for counseling because he reports having secret conversations with messengers from another planet.

   Interpersonal: 1 2 3 4 5 6 7 8 9 10
   Intercultural: 1 2 3 4 5 6 7 8 9 10
   Psychopathological: 1 2 3 4 5 6 7 8 9 10

10. A woman sees a counselor because she feels that she has a lot of difficulty making friends.

    Interpersonal: 1 2 3 4 5 6 7 8 9 10
    Intercultural: 1 2 3 4 5 6 7 8 9 10
    Psychopathological: 1 2 3 4 5 6 7 8 9 10

11. A man seeks help in trying to understand his teenage son's fixation with rock music. It appears that his son has trouble with absenteeism at school.

    Interpersonal: 1 2 3 4 5 6 7 8 9 10
    Intercultural: 1 2 3 4 5 6 7 8 9 10
    Psychopathological: 1 2 3 4 5 6 7 8 9 10

12. A man approaches a counselor with feelings of depression. He feels that his job is leading nowhere and that his occupational efforts are fruitless.

    Interpersonal: 1 2 3 4 5 6 7 8 9 10
    Intercultural: 1 2 3 4 5 6 7 8 9 10
    Psychopathological: 1 2 3 4 5 6 7 8 9 10

13. A 19-year-old sophomore complaints to a counselor that she is being sexually harassed by her male professors. She claims that this has occurred throughout her academic life.

    Interpersonal: 1 2 3 4 5 6 7 8 9 10
    Intercultural: 1 2 3 4 5 6 7 8 9 10
    Psychopathological: 1 2 3 4 5 6 7 8 9 10

14. A 32-year-old woman is reluctant to leave her parents' home to live on her own. She feels that to do so would be to lack filial responsibility.

Interpersonal: 1 2 3 4 5 6 7 8 9 10
Intercultural: 1 2 3 4 5 6 7 8 9 10
Psychopathological: 1 2 3 4 5 6 7 8 9 10

15. A 35-year-old man sees a counselor, complaining of chest and neck pains. He has sought medical help but has been diagnosed as medically "normal."

Interpersonal: 1 2 3 4 5 6 7 8 9 10
Intercultural: 1 2 3 4 5 6 7 8 9 10
Psychopathological: 1 2 3 4 5 6 7 8 9 10

16. A 31-year-old woman has been seeing a counselor for three sessions; she has remained attentive to the counselor but has said very little about herself. She rarely volunteers any information during the sessions.

Interpersonal: 1 2 3 4 5 6 7 8 9 10
Intercultural: 1 2 3 4 5 6 7 8 9 10
Psychopathological: 1 2 3 4 5 6 7 8 9 10

17. An international student is confused about his feelings. He wishes to stay in the United States and pursue an academic career, yet his sense of nationalism and family unity have pressured him to consider returning to his native country.

Interpersonal: 1 2 3 4 5 6 7 8 9 10
Intercultural: 1 2 3 4 5 6 7 8 9 10
Psychopathological: 1 2 3 4 5 6 7 8 9 10

18. A 28-year-old woman is referred by her husband because she is constantly using prescription drugs to help her cope with day-to-day existence; the woman is aware of her drug use but denies that it affects her family life.

Interpersonal: 1 2 3 4 5 6 7 8 9 10
Intercultural: 1 2 3 4 5 6 7 8 9 10
Psychopathological: 1 2 3 4 5 6 7 8 9 10

19. A 22-year-old woman approaches a counselor complaining that she cannot focus on relevant issues. She claims that her thinking has suddenly become "diffuse."

Interpersonal: 1 2 3 4 5 6 7 8 9 10
Intercultural: 1 2 3 4 5 6 7 8 9 10
Psychopathological: 1 2 3 4 5 6 7 8 9 10

20. A 20-year-old factory worker is referred to a counselor by his work supervisor. It appears that the man is lazy on the job and that his absenteeism is higher than average.

Interpersonal: 1 2 3 4 5 6 7 8 9 10
Intercultural: 1 2 3 4 5 6 7 8 9 10
Psychopathological: 1 2 3 4 5 6 7 8 9 10

Discuss whether students see the presenting problem as *primarily* a problem of interpersonal communication, a problem of intercultural contact, or a problem of pathology. When the measure has been used previously, there is a tendency for persons with less training and/or education to describe the presenting problem as more likely to be cultural and less likely to be pathological. Those with more training and/or education tended to describe the presenting problem as more likely to be pathological and less likely to be cultural.

Insight   Culturally different people will view the presenting problems from different perspectives.

Developed by Paul B. Pedersen, John Lewis, and James Campbell, Syracuse University. All rights reserved by James Campbell, John Lewis, and Paul B. Pedersen, Syracuse University, January 1984.

2.11
Life Styles and
Our Social Values*

Objective   Interviews to establish priorities need to rank order intercultural situations generated by a small multicultural group in terms of their "goodness" or social value. Participants will increase their knowledge about the variety of different lifestyles and social value contexts to which each client may belong.

Procedure   1. Thirteen brief character sketches were collected from teachers of multicultural schools.

2. Evaluate where they should be in relation to each other and in relation to your value system by placing each character in a box in the grid below. It is best to start by thinking of the boxes as four vertical columns (the characters in + + are temporarily thought of as rather equal in goodness and so on). Later, it is interesting to think of each box as varying in degrees, with the upper-left-hand corner reserved for the very best character and the lower right for the very worst. You may omit one of the 13 cases if you wish, as not fitting these categories.

1 + +	2 +	3 −	4 − −

---

* Substitute situations from your own setting.

3. The characters: It is best to receive "just enough" information about them. Do not wonder about extenuating circumstances with each of them. Make decisions with the information given.

Persistent Student

Kevin, a 14-year-old seventh grader, had hounded his SSP teacher for a recommendation to job status. He expressed a deep concern for his needs as related to needing a job. On the particular day he was taken to his job site, his *initial* question at the interview was "Can I have today off?" A youth meeting was being held that afternoon.

Quiet Student

This student is very quiet when in any kind of trouble. She is very much liked by her peers. Her grades are semi-poor because of attendance. She is sometimes very neat and appealing when she wants to be.

Encapsulated Teacher

This particular teacher, like many other teachers, has had limited exposure to cultural values other than his own. However, he has taught children from cultures other than his own for many years and considers himself well-qualified and equipped to teach these students in the same manner as the children from his own culture. His common remark is that he minimizes the differences and treats everyone as a human being.

Psychology Teacher

This teacher of psychology trained in Minnesota and has worked in administrative positions, among others, with Veterans Administration hospitals and neuropsychiatric clinics. He is in his 40s and teaches on the use of projective techniques in psychological treatment.

Responsible Teacher

My high school principal taught me what the word "responsibility" meant. He was counseling me at the time and I did not realize it. I rated him after I reached maturity as the best principal and the best teacher I have had so far in my 14 years of schooling.

Inexperienced Teacher

Although he has no teaching experience, he is very likeable. Being born in a state where two large Indian reservations are located has been his main exposure to American Indian Culture and now he is teaching American Indian culture and writing units.

Taskmaster Teacher

The job developer, whose responsibility it is to place and keep students at job stations, always takes the side of or represents the employer at the job station and assumes that fault for any failure to succeed in the job lies with the student. His "WASP" work ethic biases are sufficiently strong and dogmatically expressed that he does not encourage students to confide in him. The student tends just not to show up.

Rules-Oriented Teacher

I think that a teacher who sends a student to the office for saying "Hell (or Damn), I am not going to do that test" without asking what's wrong, without talking it over with him or her, is not really doing his/her job.

Older Teacher   She has been in the district for 20 years and graduated from the school she works in. However, she does not interact with or live in the community. She tends toward traditional education and resists innovative change.

Discouraged Student   Jim is a fair student. He does most of his work. His trouble is that he will stop doing any work where he thinks that he will not succeed.

Smart Student   A young girl is smart, quiet, and shy, but in the right situation she will open up and pour out her problems. The right situation is when she has been around the other person long enough to feel comfortable and trusting of that person.

Aggressive Student   A highly aggressive student is usually from a broken home, failing in school, in trouble with the school officials, and generally causing trouble in the classroom.

Daydreaming Student   This is a student who does not pay close attention, commonly seems to be daydreaming, seldom answers questions verbally, wastes time in class, does not hand in assignments even though they are easy for the other students, and does not seem either happy or satisfied with school.

Reflect on the choices you made. Discuss choices made by others in your group.

Did I have to deliberate a long time?

Which persons were most difficult to rank?

What does this tell me about my value system?

What ideas do I have about good and bad?

Do I have a stable value system or does it fluctuate—change with whim, etc.?

Whom do I respect? What do I respect?

Would it have made a difference if any of the characters had been of the opposite sex?

What race did you assume the characters were? Caucasians? Blacks? Indians?

What role does your value system play in your work at the university?

Does every student or problem get the same attention? Do you honestly reveal your preference? Does it make any difference?

Insight   Each individual has many different cultural roles.

PART

III

Structured
Exercises and
Experiences
to Increase
Skill

The third set of exercises focuses on increasing the interviewer's appropriate skill for making changes. Based on accurate awareness and meaningful comprehension, these exercises will guide the interviewer toward appropriate interventions with the client. The exercises provide a safe setting for the interviewer to practice actually making decisions and directing change in a variety of ways. Although not all of these exercises are rehearsals of interviewing, they provide skills that will be important to the interviewer in the context of a decisional interview.

3.1
A Classroom Debate

Objective   An interviewer will need to recognize the polarized perspectives in each cultural context and will participate in an "internalized debate" looking at each perspective, on the one hand . . . and on the other hand as well. Participating in a debate will help the interviewer increase his or her skill in taking different and contrasting perspectives.

Procedure   A two-sided topic or question is identified from the chapter or from some application of concepts in the chapter. Divide into two groups and give a week or more to prepare for a debate. The debate between two groups should be organized into a sequence of activities to structure the interaction.

It is not necessary for the group to actually believe in the point of view it is presenting, although believing in the issue will no doubt enhance motivation. *It is important to spend time preparing for the arguments and collecting supporting data to present during the debate.* An example topic for a debate might be the following:

- Side One (S1): Cultural differences need more emphasis to define one's culture in *specific* terms that highlight the *separate* identity of each group.
- Side Two (S2): Cultural similarities need more emphasis to show how we are *all* bonded together toward *shared* goals and responsibilities irrespective of differences.

Format of the debate:

(S1)   One side presents opening arguments with three members each giving a *3-minute* statement.

(S2)   The other side presents opening arguments with three members each giving a *3-minute* statement.

(S1)   The first team has *3 minutes* for rebuttal.

(S2)   The second team has *3 minutes* for a rebuttal.

(S1)   The first team has *3 minutes* for a second rebuttal.

(S2)   The second team has *3 minutes* for a second rebuttal.

(S1)   The first team has *5 minutes* for a conclusion.

(S2)   The second team has *5 minutes* for a conclusion.

Scoring of the debate is done by the rest of the class.

Scoring criteria: Rate each team on each scale with 1 = low, 10 = high

S1	S2	
___	___	1. analytical skill
___	___	2. clarity of argument and position
___	___	3. sophistication of argument
___	___	4. integration of theory and practice
___	___	5. relation of argument to reported research
___	___	6. relation of argument to current events
___	___	7. effective presentation skills
___	___	8. general effort involved by the team
___	___	9. innovative and creative ideas
___	___	10. ability to work within the stated time limits

Insight   There are at least two sides to every culturally defined issue.

Designed by Anne Pedersen, Syracuse University.

3.2
The Hidden Agenda

Objective

Each interview will have a hidden agenda, whether that agenda is explicit or implicit. Interviewers on sensitive topics need to increase skill in directing the process of how different cultures manage group situations and pressures by assigning a "hidden agenda" in a training group for a safe discussion about how hidden agendas function.

Procedure

1. An instructor, knowing the members of the group, designs a list of role tasks that reflect cultural stereotypes relating to the cultural identity of persons in the group. Some of these role tasks might be to always answer in the negative, or always in the positive, or to befriend one other person, or to get into an argument with one other person, or to talk a great deal of the time, or to not talk at all.

2. Each member of the group is given a slip of paper with one role task on it. In 10 minutes, the group as a committee must make a decision on an assigned topic. For the 10 minutes, the group discusses the topic, each member performing his or her own role task.

3. No member will be informed of what role task the other members of the group were assigned, and each member will be instructed to keep others from finding out his or her role task.

4. After the 10 minutes are over, the group members can discuss what they thought the other members' role task may have been and how performance of those role tasks affected the committee's activity.

Insight

Our culturally defined "hidden agendas" influence our role in groups.

Designed by Paul B. Pedersen, Syracuse University.

3.3
Role-Playing a "Hypothetical" Problem in a Group

Objective   Sometimes, the interviewer will be interviewing more than one client at the same time. Group interviews can become less abstract by allowing the group members an opportunity to project themselves into a cross-cultural problem by assuming roles of persons involved in that problem, not necessarily their own cultural roles, rather than simply discussing a problem. The interviewer will increase skill in managing the different clients in their cultural roles.

Procedure   A problem-solving format is needed to get at an ambiguous problem or crisis area in the group's discussion, especially when the group is divided on an issue and unable to come to a resolution.

1. A group member or the facilitator asks that the group divide up into roles to "do" a cross-cultural problem, which may be from his or her own background or in some other way related to the group. A problem may have already emerged in the group discussion.

2. The group divides up available roles in working with the problem.

3. Members of the group select roles they will enact in a group role-play situation, which may be from their own culture or a contrasting culture.

4. One or more members remain in the role of an observer or referee to facilitate debriefing.

5. The members act out in their assumed roles the conflict situation of the selected problem.

6. After role-playing, members tell the group what they learned about the problem.

Insight   Multicultural problems are not obstructions when they belong to yourself.

3.4
Orientation for
a Cross-Cultural
Experience

Objective   Change-oriented interviews may need to define the kinds of roles that are important for persons new to a culture through an orientation and to learn whether their suggested solutions to problems are appropriate to their new culture. Participants will increase their skill in bringing the client into a new cultural context.

Procedure   1. Provide participants with the following list of images that persons from other cultures could manifest (others may be added). Each image is discussed and clarified by the facilitator.
- Internationalist/nationalist
- Traditionalist/progressive
- Insider/visitor guest
- Deserving/poor
- Disoriented/oriented
- Competitor
- Culture sharer
- Elite

2. Participants are to select three images they feel are most appropriate to themselves most of the time.

3. Provide participants with problems and five solutions, prepared ahead of time by the facilitator. They are to select from the five solutions the one that most appeals to them and is consistent with the three images they have already selected. Two examples of problems and solutions within the image contexts follow.

Example 1:
Insider/Visitor Guest

A foreign student had an argument with his host family. He felt that the whole family was demanding too much of his time and attention. The family in turn felt the guest was being discourteous and demanding special treatment that they would not give to their own children. The arguments became so oppressive they affected the student's grades.

Alternatives

a. I would make some excuse and leave the host family and find another place to live.

b. I would confront the host family and tell them they were taking too much of my time and tell them to give me more time to study.

c. I would rearrange my schedule and try to study more at the university and continue to let the family take up my time.

d. I would do nothing and would accept it and do my best in school.

e. Or I would . . .

Example 2:
Disoriented/Oriented

A foreign person fails in his attempt to mix socially with Americans and puts the blame on his ethnic identity. He debases the values of his own culture and rejects his countrymen, who in turn reject him. At the same time, he is not more successful in communicating with Americans. He is isolated and feels lonely.

Alternatives

a. I would accept living in a foreign country and realize I will be lonely.

b. I would seek help, preferably from other countrymen and counselors.

c. I would socialize with people from my own country and try to show them the stupidity of our values.

d. I would start over and try to mix socially with another group of Americans.

e. Or I would . . .

4. Participants discuss each other's solutions in terms of whether or not they feel the solution helps or hinders the person's image and is appropriate to the situation.

5. Roles appropriate to the problems are then assigned and the problem is role-played.

6. Following the role-playing, each person is allowed to defend his or her position and a vote is taken of all participants regarding the best overall solution.

7. Participants may then form small groups (8-10 persons) and develop their own set of problems to solve with accompanying discussion, role-playing and voting in order to rehearse solutions to their own present and future problems.

Insight   Each multicultural situation presents choices, some better and some worse.

Adapted from "Dress Rehearsal for a Cross-Cultural Experience," by R. T. Moran, Josef A. Westerhauser, and Paul B. Pedersen. *International Educational and Cultural Exchange,* Summer 1974. Used by permission.

3.5
Culture Shock Ladder Ratings and Symptom Checklist

Objective   Adjustment interviews may be needed to help students measure the presence or absence of symptoms of culture shock in their own lives. Participants will become more skillful in assessing the degree of culture shock as it might influence the outcome of a decisional interview.

Procedure   1. The ladder below represents a set of positions ranging from life at its worst (0) to life at its best (10), as you view it personally. All things considered, where on the ladder do you feel you stand personally at the present time in your various cultural roles?

Step Number

```
10 _____ 10
 9 _____  9
 8 _____  8
 7 _____  7
 6 _____  6
 5 _____  5
 4 _____  4
 3 _____  3
 2 _____  2
 1 _____  1
 0 _____  0
```

2. How often in the past two weeks or so have you experienced the following reactions or feelings? (Students should circle their responses, from 0 to 4, for each item).

	Not at All	Rarely	Occasionally	Frequently	Almost Always
Anxious (worried or fearful about something	0	1	2	3	4
Depressed (unhappy, moody)	0	1	2	3	4
Sleep problems	0	1	2	3	4
Digestion, elimination problems	0	1	2	3	4
Tired, fatigued	0	1	2	3	4
Angry, irritable, impatient	0	1	2	3	4
Lonely	0	1	2	3	4
Forgetfulness	0	1	2	3	4
Hard time concentrating	0	1	2	3	4
Feeling of being "different," not fitting in or belonging	0	1	2	3	4
Nostalgia for remembered pleasures	0	1	2	3	4

Insight   A person may be experiencing more—or less—culture shock than he or she imagines.

Ladders exercise from Thomas Coffman (1978). Adapted with permission by Thomas Coffman, TLC Books, 9 North College Avenue, Salem, VA 24153.

3.6
Perception
and Reasoning

Objective   Interviewers need to understand how perception controls descriptions of reality. Participants will increase their skill for perceiving the client's cultural perception accurately.

Procedure   We have learned to react to any new situation from our experiences with apparently similar situations in the past. No two individuals see the same situation in exactly the same way because each of us has had different experiences.

The more differences there are in our previous experiences, the more different our responses are likely to be to a new situation.

To demonstrate how different individual perceptions of the same situation might be, ask members of a group to describe what is taking place in Figure 3.6.

Insight   Perception is more important than reality for understanding people's behavior.

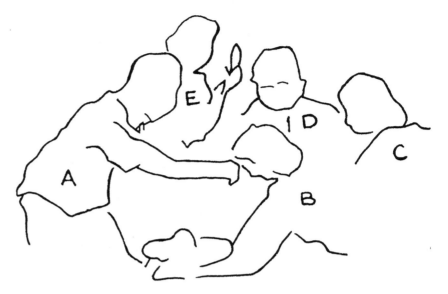

Figure 3.6
Drawing by R. Murray Thomas

3.7
Scripts for Trigger Tapes on Video

Objective
Interviewers can rehearse managing conflict by creating brief videotapes to trigger a discussion on differences. Participants will increase their skill for responding spontaneously to clients from a variety of different and dynamically changing cultural contexts.

Procedure
Ask local resource persons to make the following statements in 10- or 15-second videotapes. Fade to black after each statement.

Emotions
1. Fear Statements
   a. Don't tell my supervisor (I'm here)!
   b. My supervisor is going to have my butt when he find out I filed this complaint.
   c. There's no way I'd confront him!
   d. I can't tell my boss to get off my back!
   e. Bosses are not supposed to have these types of problems!

2. Anger
   a. Go straight to hell!
   b. If that honky ever crosses my path again, I'll kill him!
   c. I'm looking at you, know head!
   d. Every time he even comes near me I could scream!
   e. Get your act together!
   f. I could have had that job if a pretty female hadn't applied!
   g. You've always got some kind of problem.

    h. I don't care what my boss does, I'm not going back to the job!

    i. You can take this job (place) and shove it!

3. Contempt

    a. I can't stand to be near him.

    b. Don't you realize what's going on around here?

    c. You're just protecting the system and don't give a damn.

    d. What do you care, you're just like all the rest.

    e. If I had my way I'd cram all of them in this engine and blow them out the afterburner.

    f. Col Bexter is a weasel. You don't really know what I'm getting at, do you?

    g. You're reprehensible.

4. Frustration

    a. Just what do you want from me?

    b. I feel like I'm going in circles.

    c. I give up.

    d. Please repeat that and talk slower.

    e. If I see this one more time I'll scream.

    f. Why do you keep interrupting me?

    g. Man, I just got to get out of this place.

    h. Every time I suggest a new idea, I get shot down.

    i. The women in my section get away with murder.

Insight   Strong statements can trigger powerful responses across cultures.

3.8
Two Levels of Communication in the Military

Objective   Interviewers in military settings can rehearse managing conflict by identifying unspoken messages in military contexts. Participants will increase their skill in communicating with both the spoken and the unspoken messages being communicated in every decisional interview.

Procedure   Resource persons read the following script and continue spontaneously in a conversation, with feedback from the "alter ego."

1. Commander

    Commander: Our unit has the best racial climate on the base, and I'm sure you'll agree.

    Alter Ego: This should stop any further questions.

    2nd Lt: That depends on how you look at it.

    Alter Ego: Personally, I think it's the worst on base.

2. Supervisor

    Supervisor: I talk things over with my people before I act.

    Alter Ego: These people know nothing about management.

    2nd Lt: That's a good procedure to follow.

    Alter Ego: Then why am I here with the complaint in my hand?

3. Client

    Client: This supervisor I work for is always on my back about something—my work, my looks.

    Alter Ego: I know this guy is going to get me out of this.

    2nd Lt: Why do you think he's always after you?

    Alter Ego: OK, now tell me what you've done.

4. Two Social Actions personnel (Captain, Master Sergeant)

Captain: This Staff Assistance Visit will probably be a touchy situation. The Commander wants an in-depth report. Do you think you can handle it, or should I take it?

Alter Ego: I sure don't want this thing screwed up.

MSgt: Yes, I can handle it about as well as any one else.

Alter Ego: The heck with it. You think I'm going to screw it up anyway.

Insight   We communicate on many levels of meaning.

3.9
Locating Power Networks in Organizations

Objective

Power-oriented interviewers need to identify informal networks among members of a group or an organization through which power is regulated and protected. Participants will increase their skill in analyzing the importance of power networks in a group where some members are isolates and others are sought out as the interviewing context changes.

Procedure

Compose a list of all members of the group or organization. Distribute the list to all members of the group with instructions to check off the names of any other members from whom they have received help or to whom they have given help in the past week. These instructions can be revised to enlarge or reduce the focus of inquiry.

	A	B	C	D	E	F
A						
B						
C						
D						
E						
F						

Compose a code sheet with all members listed across one dimension matched to rows and the other dimension matched to columns in a matrix. Check the persons identified by each individual in the group. The final matrix should indicate both those persons selected by each member and whether or not that person was selected back in a reciprocal relationship.

If you want a visual map of these networks, draw circles for each member around the perimeter of a large sheet of paper and put one person's name in each circle. Then draw a line between those members who reciprocally identified one another. You may present this sociogram to the group for discussion on the following topics.

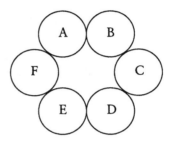

1. Which students are the "stars" in the group?
2. Who seem to be the isolates, and why?
3. Which students seem to have a strong mutual attraction for one another?
4. Which students seem to have a strong mutual rejection of one another?
5. What small groups or cliques do you see in the group?
6. Which students seem to have a strong attraction for members of other gender groups, age groups, cultural groups, etc.?
7. What age groups are represented, and what effect did this have?
8. What other information can be gathered about power networks from this sociogram?

3.10
Developing Structured Exercises For Life Skills

Objective   Additional interviewer skills can be developed by looking at areas of individual competence when interacting with host culture persons and reviewing individual abilities for intercultural awareness. Participants will increase their skill for inventing and developing exercises to increase the awareness, knowledge, and skill of others for decisional interviewing in the cultural context.

Instructions   The following examples of life skills will be related to critical incidents and to the needs or interests of the participants. Any of these skills could be related to any of the four competency areas and the target audiences as being international, interethnic, or from different role groups. Identify those skills you need to develop in a foreign culture of your choice.

1. *Interviewing:* Participants simulate both interviewing and being interviewed by persons from other cultures with an opportunity for feedback both from the other person and from a trained facilitator.

2. *Questioning:* Participants simulate likely situations (asking directions, finding out what happened, or gathering information) that require their questioning persons from another culture, with an opportunity for feedback.

3. *Comparing:* Participants learn to identify differences and similarities between themselves and persons from another culture through one-to-one discussion groups.

4. *Identifying assumptions:* Participants listen to a person from another culture describe an incident, idea, or concept and then identify the unstated assumptions that person is making about that incident, idea, or concept.

5. *Using feedback:* Participants are trained to appropriately accept and provide feedback with a person from another culture.

6. *Listening:* Participants should be able to listen closely enough to what one other person from another culture is saying that they can repeat back to that other person's satisfaction the content of what was said and some of the feelings behind that content.

7. *Skill teaching:* Participants from one culture should be able to teach participants from another culture skills necessary to communicate in their own culture.

8. *Organizing facts:* Participants should be able to organize information about another culture into a meaningful pattern of behavior that will help to understand that other culture.

9. *Describing feelings:* Participants should be able to describe their own feelings and predict what other participants will say they feel about a particular shared group experience.

10. *Fantasizing:* Participants should be able to project themselves into the role of a "problem" between persons from two cultures and role-play that fantasy appropriately.

11. *Sensitizing:* Participants should be able to identify aspects of a critical incident that persons from another culture might consider offensive and unfair.

12. *Role-playing:* Participants should be able to role-play situations they are likely to experience at some future time involving interaction with persons from another culture both in their own role and in the role of a person from that other culture.

13. *Using help:* Participants should be able to identify aspects of a critical incident where persons from another culture might appropriately help one another.

14. *Using multimedia:* Participants should be able to demonstrate ways in which pictures, music, or other media might be helpful in understanding that other culture.

15. *Contracting:* Participants should be able to identify terms of a "contract" or agreement between themselves and the life skills training program concerning those skills they wish to learn and their investment in that learning.

16. *Planning:* Participants should be able to present a plan on specific ways they expect to use their learning from the cross-cultural communications course.

17. *Using criteria:* Participants should be able to identify the criteria they use in evaluating the work of persons from another culture.

18. *Supporting others:* Participants should be able to demonstrate in simulated critical incidents how they would support persons from their own and another culture during an intercultural exchange.

19. *Deferring judgment:* Participants in a creative problem-solving exercise should be able to defer judgment on solutions being presented by persons from a variety of cultures while a comprehensive list of alternatives is being compiled.

20. *Reporting:* Participants should be able to report accurately to the satisfaction of other participants in that intercultural group.

21. *Summarizing:* Participants should be able to summarize accurately the discussion on a particular critical incident among members of their intercultural group.

22. *Problem solving with a system:* Participants should be able to identify and use appropriately the ways in which persons from different cultures approach, define, and solve problems.

Insight   Creating structured exercises to fit the particular cultural context is an important skill.   ♠

PART

IV

Critical
Incidents to
Demonstrate
Awareness,
Knowledge,
and *Skill*

The critical incident technique is closely related to the case study method, which evaluates the behavior of a person or persons in a clinical or decision-making setting, examining background, behavior, and changes in behavior over a period of months or years. Case data describe and interpret impressions about the subject from a qualitative/subjective rather than a quantitative/objective viewpoint. Sigmund Freud made the case study method the foundation of his theories, whereas Carl Rogers, Gordon Allport, and other therapists have frequently used the case study method in psychological analysis. Although cases are easier to visualize than numbers, it is difficult to generalize from cases. It is also difficult to separate cause from effect in cases. Finally, the investigator's biases and assumptions will be reflected in the cases reported. Cases are particularly useful when examining an extraordinary situation, when the subject is typical of a defined group, when the case illustrates a special method or experience, and when possibilities are being demonstrated for the future. These characteristics make critical incidents useful for conditions to the study of culture shock among people around the world.

The following critical incidents will create a variety of different cultural contexts in which decisional interviewing might be appropriate. These situations are more complex and dynamic in real-life settings than in these "safe" critical incidents through which participants can practice decisional interviewing in the cultural context. Although these critical incidents are useful for individual training and development, their usefulness would be enhanced in a class or group setting where the different perspectives of each incident become more apparent.

A major advantage of critical incidents is the focus on observable behaviors. The disadvantages are that it requires considerable time and effort to collect the incidents and to code them in a meaningful way. The incidents also tend to emphasize the extraordinary rather than the average or typical situation, which distorts or exaggerates aspects of the experience. It is sometimes hard to generalize from critical incidents to the real world. It is also difficult to get consensus about the appropriate response in a multicultural critical incident.

Critical incidents are particularly popular in teaching or training about multicultural relationships. In part, this happens because more specific and focused measures are more likely to impose a cultural bias. In part, it is because critical incidents are more open ended and include the complexity of real-life situations where persons from more than one culture come into contact. The critical incident methodology has been used to develop and to measure several multicultural competencies:

1. *Information source development:* Students develop the ability to use many information sources within a social or cultural environment. In collecting critical incidents, information-gathering skills such as observing, questioning the people one meets, and careful listening skills are developed.

2. *Cultural understanding:* Awareness and understanding of values, feelings, and attitudes of people in another culture and the ways in which these values influence behavior are clarified. Critical incidents help illustrate the ways in which values, expectations, and attitudes undergird behaviors.

3. *Interpersonal communication:* Listening well, speaking clearly, and paying attention to the expression of nonverbal communication, such as messages delivered through physical movements of eyes and face, are highlighted as important aspects of face-to-face encounters in the incidents.

4. *Commitment to persons and relationships:* Enhanced ability to become involved with people from other cultures may be developed through the process of collecting critical incidents. This involves giving and inspiring trust and confidence, establishing a basis for mutual liking and respect, caring for culturally different people, and acting in ways that are both truthful and sensitive toward the feelings of others.

5. *Decision making:* Students develop the ability to come to conclusions based on their own assessment of the information available and their identification of the right action or response. This might also be called problem solving, which includes learning to be explicit about the problem, working out steps to a solution, and generating alternatives. In the multicultural situation, it is important to identify what is at issue, the dimensions of the problem, and the alternatives that are personally and culturally available.

There is no substitute for actual experience. The critical incident technique is an attempt to bring actual experiences or events into the classroom as a resource. The incident is critical—meaning important, essential, or valuable—in the way that a part of a machine might be critical to the smooth operation of the machine. The incident is a short description of an event that took place within a 5- or 10-minute period of time. A case study, by contrast, is much more complicated and might take place over weeks, months, or even years.

Critical incidents are based on real-life situations and typically involve a dilemma where there is no easy or obvious solution. The objective of critical incidents is to stimulate thinking about basic and important issues that occur in real-life situations. By analyzing the incident, participants can imagine themselves in the same situation, develop strategies to deal with that situation, and become more realistic in their expectations. Rehearsing what a participant would do in a critical incident provides the relative safety of a training situation, requires limited risk taking, and yet provides much of the complexity of real-life situations.

Critical incidents do not necessarily imply a single solution or a "right way" of resolving the dilemma in a situation, but they explore alternative solutions and their implications or consequences. The critical incident reporting format applied by students in this project was organized into six categories:

1. Identify the event or occurrence with as much specificity as possible, the problem to be solved, the decision to be made, and the issues involved.
2. Describe the relevant details and circumstances surrounding the event so that readers will understand what happened: when, how, why, and where.
3. List the people involved, describing them and their relationships to the observer and to one another.
4. Describe the observer's own role in the situation in terms of what was done or how that person acted, identifying the particular multicultural skill or skills involved and the choices made.
5. Write a brief analysis of the incident telling what you learned from the incident, stating estimates of the observer's and actor's levels of multicultural skill development.
6. Identify the specific psychological construct or concept that is illustrated in this critical incident.

Sue and Sue (1990) have incorporated critical incidents into their book on counseling culturally different clients. Eighteen critical incidents are used to illustrate concepts of cross-cultural counseling in their book. These incidents share three characteristics: (a) Each incident illustrates a conflict of cultures, values, standards, or goals; (b) the solutions are not obvious, and the alternatives are deliberately controversial; and (c) each incident includes a description of the conditions or context in which the incident occurred. There are several reasons why Sue and Sue favor critical incidents as a methodology:

1. Trainees can learn change-agent skills early in training by identifying social, cultural, and political forces operating in each situation.
2. Critical incidents provide a laboratory for examining dangerous situations, personal biases, value differences, and sensitive issues with safety for the trainee and the client.
3. The readers are encouraged to identify as many cross-cultural issues in each incident as possible so that they can see the same situation from different perspectives.
4. The readers can identify conflicts of values among the different characters within each incident and between each character and social institution.
5. The readers are encouraged to become committed to a course of action by examining their own values and biases and by projecting their own self-reference criterion into the critical incidents.

Critical incidents have been used to do research on work motivation and satisfaction, as a work performance appraisal, and as a behavior-anchored developmental scale (Sauser, 1987). One very popular variation on critical incidents for international/intercultural training is the culture assimilator (Albert, 1983; Fiedler, Mitchell, & Triandis, 1971), where the target audience and target culture are specified and where the training is designed to match one specific culture with another specific but contrasting culture. Following each incident, the culture assimilator identifies alternative possible attributions about the behaviors from the host culture point of view, with one set of attributions being more accurate than the others.

Fiedler et al. (1971) describe an ideal critical incident for the culture assimilator as being (a) a typical interaction between two cultures, (b) apparently conflictful, puzzling and open to misinterpretation, (c) a situation in which a right decision could be made if all relevant information were available, and (d) a situation that is relevant to a specific task, mission, or training objective. The culture assimilator is adaptable to a wide variety of multicultural settings. If the incidents are gathered by sensitive observers, they can reflect a great deal of cultural complexity and understanding. The research supporting culture assimilators suggests that the following benefits result from its use:

1. Greater understanding of hosts, as judged by the hosts themselves
2. A decrease in the use of negative stereotypes on the part of trainees
3. The development of complex thinking about the target culture, which replaces the oversimplified, facile thinking to which hosts react negatively
4. Greater enjoyment among trainees who interact with members of the target culture, a feeling reciprocated by hosts
5. Better adjustment to the everyday stresses of life in other cultures
6. Better job performance in cases where performance is influenced by specific cultural practices that can be covered in the training materials

Brislin, Cushner, Cherrie, and Yang (1986) have developed a general culture assimilator not directed toward a specific bicultural relationship but toward a more general and unspecified target audience. These materials were developed to help people adjust to any other culture. Brislin and his colleagues identified 100 critical incidents according to nine broad categories:

1. The historical myths people brought with them to another culture
2. People's attitudes, traits, and skills
3. Their thought and attribution processes
4. The groups they join

5. The range of situations in which they have to interact
6. Their management of cross-cultural conflict
7. The tasks they want to accomplish
8. The organizations of which they are a part
9. The process of short- and long-term adjustments

The emphasis in this general culture assimilator approach is to avoid thinking of a particular target culture but rather focus on the participant's own internal and intrapsychic state. This approach emphasizes commonalities across cultures. The culture-specific and the general culture assimilators supplement one another in training. Although the general culture assimilator cannot be precisely accurate to a particular bicultural relationship, Brislin et al. advocate the general assimilator under five different conditions.

1. When a culture-specific training program is not available
2. To provide a basis for covering culture-specific information in newly developed programs by guiding resource persons in their training of sojourners
3. To integrate a great deal of specific information without overwhelming the participant
4. To encourage the development of a multicultural perspective across cultures.
5. To provide a way to involve students in courses through specific incidents and examples.

4.1
Critical Incidents Involving Ethnic Minorities

Diagram the conflict between culturally different persons in each of the following brief critical incidents using the Interpersonal Cultural Grid to find examples of "common ground" where the two individuals shared the same *positive* expectations but expressed their expectation in culturally *different* behaviors.

The Interpersonal Cultural Grid (Figure 4.1) is an attempt to describe the relationship between persons or groups by separating behaviors from expectations. The Interpersonal Cultural Grid has four quadrants, each of which explains one large or small part of a relationship between two individuals or groups. Salience may change from one quadrant to the other as the relationship changes.

| | | **Behaviors** | |
		Same	Different
Expectations	Same or Positive	1 Peace	2 Cross-cultural Positive Conflict
	Different or Negative	3 Personal Negative Conflict	4 War

Figure 4.1

97

In the first quadrant, two individuals have similar behaviors and similar positive expectations. There is a high level of accuracy in both individuals' interpretations of one another's behavior and the positive shared expectations behind that behavior. This aspect of the relationship is congruent and probably harmonious. Both persons are smiling, and both persons expect friendship.

In the second quadrant, two individuals have different behaviors but share the same positive expectations. There is a high level of agreement in that both persons expect trust and friendliness, but there is a low level of accuracy because each person perceives and incorrectly interprets the other's behavior as different, probably hostile. This quadrant is characteristic of multicultural conflict where each person is applying a self-reference criterion to interpret the other person's behavior. The conditions described in Quadrant 2 are very unstable, and, unless the shared positive expectations are quickly made explicit, the salience is likely to change toward Quadrant 3. It is important for at least one of the two persons to capture the conflict in this second quadrant, where the persons may agree to disagree or adapt to one another without feeling threatened because they both have shared positive expectations.

In the third quadrant, the two persons have the same behaviors but now they have different expectations, and at least one of them probably has a negative expectation for the relationship. The similar behaviors give the appearance of harmony and agreement, but the hidden different or negative expectations may destroy the relationship. One person may continue to expect trust and friendliness, whereas the other person is now negatively distrustful and unfriendly even though they are both presenting smiling and glad-handing behaviors. If these two persons discover that the reason for their conflict is a difference of expectation, they may be able to return to Quadrant 2 and reverse the escalating conflict between them. If the difference in expectations is ignored or undiscovered, the conflict eventually moves to the fourth quadrant.

The fourth quadrant is where the two people have different and/or negative expectations and they stop pretending to behave in congruent ways. The two persons are "at war" with one another and may not want to increase harmony in their relationship any longer. This relationship is likely to result in hostile disengagement. It is very difficult to retrieve conflict from the fourth quadrant because one or both parties has stopped trying to mediate or reduce the conflict.

Although the behaviors are relatively easy to identify as congruent/similar or incongruent/dissimilar, it is much more difficult to identify the expectations accurately. First, multicultural conflict might be based on misattributions and misperceptions, but both parties respond to their perception of reality, whether true or not. Second, there is a lack of reliable or complete information about what others expect, resulting in partisan or self-serving expectations by both parties. Third, both culturally different parties typically have stereotyped expectations about one another rather than accurate data. Fourth, any perceived inaccuracy or inappropriateness in assessing the other person's expectations may destroy the relationship. Fifth, selective perception, attributional distortion, and self-fulfilling prophecies might increase rather than decrease conflict.

For example, smiling is an ambiguous behavior. It may imply trust and friendliness, or it may not. The smile may be interpreted accurately, or it may not. Outside of its learned context, the smile has no fixed meaning. The example of smiling provides a means to apply the four types of interaction to distinguish among ideal, multicultural, personal, and hostile alternatives.

Examples of Critical Incidents

1. At a rally protesting the lack of Black, Hispanic, and Native American professors at a state university campus, students gathered and listened to speakers as they expressed their concerns of inequalities. The rally was a part of a week of events creating cultural awareness in higher education. Issues discussed centered around the slow recruitment of minority professors, admissions standards that were biased against minorities, and the lack of ethnic studies on campus.

   The rally received a great turnout. Minority students applauded and cheered as the lectures continued. Nonminority students began gathering at the rally listening to the many speeches being delivered. A Hispanic male, excited at seeing a large nonminority population attend the rally, commented to a student, "I'm glad to see you attend the rally. It makes me feel good to see you support our cause." The White student turned and said, "These issues of inequality are important to me." "Being Jewish has not always been easy," replied the student.

2. A Hispanic couple living in California hired a live-in nanny to care for their two daughters. The nanny, a 19-year-old undocumented immigrant, came to California to seek employment in order to earn money and help pay for a surgery that her ill father needed. The Hispanic couple were both professionals; the husband was an educator and the wife worked in marketing in the computer industry.

   One day the couple informed the nanny that the family would be relocating to the East Coast in three months. The nanny declined to move with the family, feeling insecure leaving a large Hispanic population and fearing that the move would bring her in closer contact with immigration agents at state borders.

   Two weeks prior to leaving, the couple located a job for the nanny working for another family. The nanny was excited about securing another family to care for but expressed that readjusting to another environment was difficult for her. Complicating matters further was the fact that the new family spoke little Spanish. A month after relocating to the East Coast, the couple received notice from their former nanny that her younger sister had been killed in an auto accident. The nanny was faced with many hardships—adjusting to a nonbilingual family, not having saved enough money for her father's surgery, and now the loss of her sister. Referral to free counseling services were made; however, she refused on the basis of trust and fear of deportation. Two weeks later, the nanny suffered a nervous breakdown and was hospitalized.

3. A Mexican-American doctoral student interviewing for a graduate assistantship position in a student service program was having a conversation with the director of the retention program. The director discussed the role and responsibility of the assistantship position. The primary responsibility would be outreach targeted specifically toward Hispanic students on campus who were not utilizing the services that were available to them. The director believed that the doctoral student would be a good role model for the Hispanic students, and hopefully these students would utilize the services more frequently.

During the course of the interview the director stated that he believes that, due to biological factors, some people were able to learn more and were more intelligent than others. The director informed the doctoral student that he wanted to be open and honest to avoid uneasiness down the road.

4. Susan, a White female at a small liberal arts college, recently ended a three-year relationship with her high school boyfriend. Her roommate, Jill, noticed that Susan began sleeping in and eating less. Jill believed that this type of behavior was just a phase Susan was going through and that soon she would be her self again.

One night after returning from a late night movie, Jill noticed a small container of pills on Susan's nightstand. Jill shared her concerns about the pills with Susan and recommended that she seek free counseling available through the campus counseling center. Susan replied that she had thought about counseling but felt uncomfortable because the counselors at the center were all males and she preferred to meet with a female counselor.

5. A Vietnamese high school student was experiencing difficulty concentrating on her schoolwork due to issues at home. Hesitant in talking to someone about family issues, she felt she had no choice but to meet with her school counselor as her studies were suffering.

The Vietnamese student informed the counselor that due to financial hardships her father had started drinking and had become physically violent toward the family. The student also stated that she was staying up late at night comforting her three-year-old sister who was scared and had regressed to bed-wetting.

The counselor expressed that she was saddened to hear of the situation and conveyed to the student the importance of continuing school so that she could go on to college, graduate, and help contribute at home by helping out financially. The counselor informed the student that her situation was common of recent immigrants and tried to assure her that things would get better.

6. A Chinese-American transferring to a four-year university was invited to an orientation for new students. The new students were given a schedule of spring classes and instructed to tentatively select their classes and then meet with the department adviser for approval.

After completing the instructions, the Chinese-American met with his adviser. As he left the adviser's office, the adviser said, in an effort to welcome the student, "You know, the restaurant across the street sells the best won ton soup around."

7. A Taiwanese student returned to her home country after receiving her graduate degree in counseling in the United States. Her initial work consisted of explaining the process on counseling and how counseling was used in the United States. Many of her contacts could not believe that Americans would tell their personal stories to a stranger and how that stranger was paid to listen.

After a short period in Taiwan, the student returned to the United States in hopes of working as a counselor in a university setting. She explained that it was difficult to do counseling in a culture that did not believe in discussing personal or family matters outside their home.

8. A 50-year-old Mexican woman was referred to a counselor by her physician. The referral was made after the woman related her chest pains to being unable to attend her mother's funeral. The counselor, a Mexican American, learned that the woman did not receive notice of her mother's death until months later, as her family in Mexico had no phone.

The counselor assessed that her pain was caused by the guilt she carried. The counselor also learned that the woman had no family or relatives nearby. To address her needs, the counselor contacted a local parish that gave mass in Spanish; he spoke with the priest and informed him of the situation. The priest said that he was able to meet with the woman that afternoon.

A few weeks later, the Mexican woman contacted the counselor and thanked him for his help. The woman said that the priest was able to have a rosary and a mass for her mother.

9. A Chinese graduate student recently finished his master's degree in counseling psychology and was preparing to apply to a doctoral program. The student received many invitations to attend numerous universities throughout the country and also received fellowship offers from several prestigious universities.

   The Chinese student visited the doctoral programs at universities that were within reasonable driving distance. For universities that were out of state, the student was able to do research through the mail.

   After narrowing the selection to five universities, the student met with his adviser to decide on which school to attend. After a lengthy conversation with his adviser, the student finally made a decision. One important factor that he had overlooked, however, was that none of the five schools had faculty of color, specifically professors of Chinese decent.

10. Maria, a 17-year-old first-generation Mexican American high school student, was angry and upset because she was not given permission to attend a field trip to visit a local university. Maria's friends were concerned about her behavior and informed a counselor at the Counseling and Guidance Center. The counselor, a female Mexican American, met with Maria to find out what was troubling her. Maria explained that she would like to attend college but that her family did not support her decision. Maria mentioned that her father wanted her to stay home and help her mother around the house and that maybe in a few years when she was older she could possibly go on to school. Maria believed her father's real reason for not being supportive of her continuing her education was due to the rapes that were occurring on college campuses.

    Ms. Bustamante shared with Maria that she too was not supported by her parents when she went to college. She, however, was not angry at her parents because she knew that her parents really loved her, and she found a way to convey to her parents the benefits of attending college.

    Ms. Bustamante advised Maria to do the same and suggested that she share with her parents information about the different colleges. Ms. Bustamante also suggested that Maria gather information about housing and, if possible, the security services the campuses offer students.

11. A counselor at an urban high school was leaving his office after school to meet with a teacher in another building. As he approached the school library he heard two people screaming and shouting. The counselor went to see what the commotion was all about and witnessed a Vietnamese mother hitting a young Vietnamese female with an umbrella. The counselor immediately stopped the woman from hitting the student and escorted them to the administration office.

Mrs. Troung, a volunteer teacher's aide, was called in to assist with the matter. After a long discussion with the mother and student, Mrs. Troung shared with the counselor the following: The older Vietnamese woman was the mother of the student. She was upset because the daughter had told the mother she was studying at the school library and that was why she had arrived home late for the past several nights. Today, the mother came to the school to make sure her daughter was studying. Upon arriving at the school, the mother found her daughter talking with a Vietnamese boy and began hitting her for lying. The parent's rule was that the daughter was not to have a boyfriend until she was ready to marry.

12. An Asian family met with a family therapist because the parents were having difficulty controlling their oldest son. The parents were immigrants and were referred to family services via a community agency. The therapist, a Hispanic female, was experiencing difficulty establishing a smooth session. Although she was aware of the cultural factors in counseling Asian families, she realized that for some reason the session did not go as well as she wanted.

    As the session came to an end, the therapist scheduled them for the following week. A couple of days later the family canceled their appointment and asked if they could have a referral. The therapist asked if she had upset them in any way and the mother responded that she did not; however, she did comment that her husband would feel more comfortable if the therapist were an older Asian male.

13. Jessica, a 22-year-old Mexican American female from central Illinois, left home to attend college in California. A few weeks into the semester, she began to notice the cultural difference between herself and other Hispanics on campus. Jessica noticed that the majority of the Hispanics were able to speak both English and Spanish fluently. Although her parents spoke Spanish at home, it was not mandatory that the children be bilingual.

    In her English class, which was composed of predominantly White students, Jessica felt comfortable and relaxed. However, in a Chicano Studies course that fulfilled the cultural pluralism requirement for graduation, she felt out of place because she did not share the same types of experiences as other Hispanics in class.

    Jessica shared her feelings with the Chicano Studies professor who was very sensitive to her issue. The professor responded by telling Jessica that not all Mexican Americans share the same sociocultural experience and that people need to understand and respect the values of others.

14. Raquel, a 29-year-old Hispanic college student, recently received her bachelor of arts degree in English. Raquel graduated with

honors and was the first of seven siblings to finish college. Raquel was married and had two children, ages 2 and 4. Her husband worked the swing shift at a supermarket, and she worked as a teacher's aide at an elementary school. During the day, Raquel's husband would take care of the children, and in the afternoon, he would leave them with his mother. Raquel attended classes three nights a week, and after class she would pick up the children.

A couple of weeks prior to graduation, Raquel was informed about an award that she had been nominated for by the faculty in her department. The award recognized outstanding students in Comparative English Literature. The department chair met with Raquel to discuss graduate school. She was offered a scholarship to attend the master's program in English the following fall.

Raquel was torn between graduate school and being at home with her children. After several days of thinking about the offer, she decided that she would take a year off from school so that she could be with her family. Coincidentally, Raquel did not receive the award for which she had been nominated.

15. Leonard, a Lakota Indian, returned home to the reservation after serving three years in the armed services. During his stay in the Marine Corps, he was stationed at several bases in the United States and was sent to Germany for a one-year period. At a sweat lodge, many of Leonard's friends and older members of the tribe shared stories of their ancestors. When Leonard was a child he remembered listening to his father tell stories about his great-grandfather and how he always enjoyed learning about his family history. However, Leonard noticed that now these stories did not mean anything to him and that he could not understand the importance that his tribe placed in talking about individuals who no longer existed.

After several weeks at home from the service, Leonard found himself in conflict with his parents and siblings. Many of his friends claimed that Leonard was acting as though he was too good to be a Lakota Indian. The conflict between family and friends caused Leonard much pain. He felt that no one understood him. He felt alone. Leonard wanted to leave the reservation to find work so that he could save his money and travel through Europe; however, he knew that with only a high school education getting a job would be difficult.

Leonard became more depressed about the conflict that he was experiencing at home. He realized he could no longer live on the reservation and be happy. After two months at home, Leonard left the reservation and reenlisted in the Marines for another full term.

16. In "Silent Language," Edward T. Hall talked about his experience working for the soil conservation program at a Navajo reservation.

While supervising the construction of small earth dams, he noticed that the Navajo workmen operated in a relaxed pace as though they had no worries at all. He recalls sharing his American values about the hard work ethic and that working hard today will bring rewards tomorrow. Hall noticed that this did not bring about changes in their work behavior.

After discussing this problem with a friend who lived all his life on a reservation, Hall decided to approach the Navajo workmen in a different manner. He recalls talking with the work crew and telling them how the "American government was giving them money to get out of debt by providing them jobs near their families and giving them water for their sheep." Hall stressed the fact that in return they had to work hard 8 hours a day. He noticed that the change in approaches altered their work performance.

17. A Middle Eastern student attending a university on the East Coast was experiencing a difficult time meeting American students. One day after his chemistry class, he decided to talk with a student who sat next to him in class. The classmate was an American female who easily engaged in a conversation with the Middle Eastern student. After a few minutes of conversing, the American student on several occasions glanced at her watch. The Middle Eastern student noticed her behavior and felt as though he was intruding or boring her with his conversation.

On another occasion, the Middle Eastern student was having lunch at the campus cafeteria. While he was eating, he noticed that many American students were eating and reading at the same time. Others were eating and writing letters or doing their schoolwork. He found it very interesting that American students rarely relaxed.

18. Pélin, an international student from Taiwan, was asked to share her experience with students who had recently arrived in the United States from China. Pélin shared that when she first arrived she was excited about attending an American university. In her spare time she went to see American movies and ate a variety of American foods. After some time, she began noticing the major differences in the behavior of American students and how their beliefs, values, and lifestyle conflicted with hers.

Pélin lived in the residential halls and had an American roommate. She spoke of how offended and embarrassed she was when her roommate's boyfriend came by to visit and how openly they would kiss and hug each other. She also shared the difficulty she experienced when using the community showers for women. Her sense of privacy and personal space was constantly being challenged.

Pélin shared with the group that, at first, her adjustment as a student at an American university was difficult, and although many of the values were different from hers, she was able to adjust. Pélin ended in saying that her biggest growth was being able to appreciate her values by learning to appreciate American values.

19. An admissions counselor at a California state university was reviewing an admissions application submitted by a Vietnamese refugee student. Sections of the admissions application requested parental information and specific questions about the family history. Because these sections were left blank, the student was requested to make an appointment with the admissions counselor.

     During their meeting, the counselor learned that the student and his sister were living with an aunt and they had no knowledge of the existence of their parents. The student hesitantly shared with the counselor that his parents were taken as prisoners by the communist regime in Vietnam and he was left behind with his younger sister. Through VIA, the refugee program, he was able to locate his aunt in California.

     It had been 10 years since he had seen his parents. The student expressed that it was important for him to go to college because with a college degree he would be able to take care of his younger sister and not be such a burden to his aunt.

20. A Hispanic social worker in Colorado was assigned a client who had been raped by her employer. The client was a 25-year-old Mexican woman who came to the United States so that she could work and save money to pay for an operation her son needed.

     The client had answered an ad in the paper to work as a live-in nanny. The employer was a successful dentist, who was married and had two children. Within days after the Mexican woman had started working, she was raped by the dentist. Unable to speak English and fearful of the consequences of deportation, the woman could not report the incident to authorities.

     In desperation, she went to see a priest for help. The priest contacted a clinic who later contacted the social work agency. It was discovered that the woman had been raped on 11 different occasions within a 5-day period.

21. A counselor at a rehabilitation center for juveniles was assigned to a case in which the minor had a history of aggressive behavior. The minor was sent to the rehabilitation center for 8 months because of his prior history and violation of probation. After a few counseling sessions, the counselor and the minor were able to identify situations that caused him to act in an aggressive manner. It was learned in the counseling session that the minor as a young child witnessed his father physically abuse his mother. The minor described his father as a man who had a short fuse and vented his anger at his mother.

The minor internalized his feelings and developed an intense hatred toward his father. The minor grew up not knowing how to deal with his anger and would act out when confronted with stressful situations. Through additional counseling, it was discovered that the minor had an uncle he respected very highly and always called whenever he was in trouble. The minor shared with the counselor that his uncle was someone who was always there when he needed someone to talk with. The uncle was his mother's older brother who was self-employed and often traveled.

Through further counseling, the minor and the counselor were able to develop strategies in dealing with the minor's behavior when confronted with stressful situations. Rewards were granted in the form of additional visitation time with his mother on Sundays when the minor was able to control his anger. The minor received training in breathing exercises to help him control his emotions in a stressful event. The counselor also arranged special visitations with the minor's uncle and worked with the minor's mother in learning prosocial skills in preparation for his release.

22. A married couple met with a counselor to discuss the difficulties they were having with their oldest daughter. The daughter was 15 years old and a sophomore in high school. The parents' primary concern was that their daughter was always yelling at them and was in total control of her life. The parents' concern was that they had no control over their own daughter.

    The counselor spoke to the parents in detail about areas that could be worked on; however, it required that the parents participate in the learning and training of anger control skills. The parents were very hesitant and shared with the counselor that it would be difficult to actively take part in the process.

23. In a small community in Texas, parents of Mexican American children were upset when several of the students were placed in a specialized classroom designed for learning disabilities. Several parents received a letter from the teacher stating that their child had been given a standardized intelligence test and the results were very low.

    The letter stated that the exam provided evidence that their child was borderline mentally retarded. After much pressure from the parents, consultants from a university evaluated the exam and found that the intelligence test was biased. The test itself did not take into account both linguistic and cultural factors of the students who were tested.

    The students were retested with an intelligence test that was not biased and was sensitive to linguistic and cultural elements. The results of the exam indicated that the Mexican American students did not differ from White Anglo students and in several areas scored higher than their Anglo counterparts.

24. An African American woman met with a counselor because she was feeling depressed about being unemployed. The client expressed that she felt worthless and useless. Unemployed for the past four months, she could not understand why with a business degree and four years of professional experience she had been unable to find a job.

    The client stated that for the past three months she had been sending out six résumés a week and had not received any responses. The woman began questioning her own ability and self-confidence and began to feel that she did not have the right stuff.

25. A White female school counselor recently moved to Los Angeles from Ohio with her husband, who had accepted a principal's position at a high school. The counselor experienced culture shock when she met the parents of a Hispanic student who were concerned about their son's truancy problem. The parents spoke limited English but sufficient enough to be able to communicate with those who did not speak Spanish.

    Understanding the demographics of the school where the counselor worked and in anticipation of working with Hispanic parents who were limited-English-speaking, the counselor thought it beneficial to enroll in a Spanish class at a community college near her residence. She did so for the following six months.

    At work, the counselor would practice her Spanish with students whenever possible and found that Hispanic students were less inhibited around her. On several occasions, the counselor was able to speak Spanish with parents who spoke limited English. She noticed that by speaking Spanish with the parents they felt relaxed and comfortable. The counselor realized that by being able to communicate in the language of her clients she was able to establish trust and rapport.

26. An Asian family who was experiencing difficulty with their oldest daughter met with a family therapist. The family informed the counselor that they did not approve of their daughter having boyfriends and found it difficult getting her to obey their rules.

    The therapist spoke with the parents about relationships and what that meant to a teenage female. The therapist informed the parents it would probably be best if the daughter could attend their next meeting so they could all work out a solution together.

    The parents were somewhat taken back by what the therapist had told them and expressed that they did not think it was possible for the family to meet. All they wanted was for the therapist to tell them how to handle the situation.

4.2

Introductory Seminar in Intercultural Communication Skills for Help Providers in the Military

The U.S. military represents an extremely large concentration of U.S. nationals in an international context under conditions where contact with host nationals and culturally different coworkers might occur under less than favorable conditions. For this reason, it is important to provide favorable structures wherever possible for intercultural communication to occur.

Cross-cultural training approaches have developed a variety of structures that can facilitate favorable conditions for intercultural contact. Besides contact between different nationality and ethnic groups, there is also a great diversity within the military that requires intercultural structures for accurate communication and informed assessment. In previous cross-cultural training with the military, it has become apparent that differences in rank, roles, and service branch function in ways similar to culture groups and require many of the same intercultural skills for communication. Other differences of age, sex role, lifestyle, socioeconomic status, and affiliations further complicate the cultural patterns of culturally different service persons.

Intercultural Communication Barriers

There are several ICC barriers that can create misunderstanding.

1. First, there is the obvious barrier of *LANGUAGE DIFFERENCES.* Language is much more than learning new sound symbols. Knowing a little of the foreign language may only allow you to make a "fluent fool" of yourself.

2. Second, there is the area of *NONVERBAL COMMUNICATION,* such as gestures, postures, and other ways we communicate what we feel and think. Our culture has taught us to communicate what we feel and think. Our culture has taught us to communicate through "unspoken" messages that are sometimes so automatic that we do not even think about them. A counselor might put his or her own cultural interpretation on your hand gesture, facial expression, posture, clothing, touching, eye contact, or personal appearance that was not what you intended at all.

3. *PRECONCEPTIONS AND STEREOTYPES* provide a third barrier where we try to fit people into patterns based on our previous experience with them. We see pretty much what we want to or expect to and reject the possible interpretations that do not fit with what we expect. When the counselor first becomes aware of another culture, these half-formed stereotypes are most likely to betray communication. If you expect a particular culture to behave in a particular way, there is a stronger likelihood that you will interpret their behavior in that way.

4. A fourth barrier is a *TENDENCY TO EVALUATE BEHAVIORS* from the other culture, as good or bad, making a judgment based on our own cultural bias. Earlier in this unit we mentioned that different attitudes about social customs, family life, food, drink, and toilet etiquette, roles and role expectations, religions, and folk beliefs are cultural differences you will most likely encounter on the airplane and can cause misunderstanding.

5. A fifth barrier is the typically *HIGH LEVEL OF STRESS* that accompanies intercultural communication. Like every other unfamiliar experience, intercultural contact is likely to involve some stress.

Ways to Decrease Intercultural Communication Barriers

1. Language
   a. Learn the language.
   b. Find someone who can speak the language.
   c. Ask for clarification if you are not sure what the person said.
2. Nonverbal Communication
   a. Do not assume you understand any nonverbal communication unless you are familiar with the culture.
   b. If the nonverbal communication is insulting in your culture, do not take it personally.

    c. Develop an awareness of your own nonverbal communication that might be insulting in certain cultures.

  3. Preconceptions and Stereotypes

    a. Make every effort to increase awareness of your own preconceptions and stereotypes of cultures you encounter.

    b. With this awareness, reinterpret their behavior from their cultural perspective.

    c. *Be willing to test, adapt, and change your own stereotypes* to fit your new experiences.

  4. Evaluation of Behavior

    a. Maintain objectivity.

    b. Recognize that you cannot change a culture overnight.

    c. Do not judge someone from another culture by your own cultural values until you have come to know them and their cultural values first.

  5. Stress

    Cross-cultural situations are often ambiguous and result in stress because we are not sure what others expect of us or what we can expect of them. As intercultural barriers are reduced, you can expect the level of stress to diminish.

Instruction   In each situation, you will first be given a description of an actual event that took place.

Second, you will be asked to identify which ICC barriers are relevant to this situation.

Third, you will be asked to provide several responses to the situation and select those responses that are the most appropriate.

Rank Order Responses   Choose the response(s) that have the best possible consequences for the complainant and the other person(s), thereby being likely to decrease the ICC barriers. Explain why you chose these response(s).

1. (What I would *like* to do.)
2. (What I *should* do).
3. (What I would actually do.)

Identify the ICC barriers that should be considered in selecting a response to the situation:

1. Language:
2. Nonverbal:
3. Stereotypes:
4. Evaluation:
5. Stress:

1. Sexual Harassment

    Complainant: CMS White male

    Offender: White female secretary

    Complainant: A secretary in my office has lodged a sexual harassment complaint against me with the civilian EEO. She claims I sexually harassed her by using endearing terms and derogatory comments. She lodged this complaint yesterday based on a statement I made that she claims was offensive. The statement was made in pure jest. She usually carries a key to the duplication machine which is tied to a large metal hook. She appeared to be in a good mood, I was in a good mood, so I said, "Hey, here comes my favorite hooker." There were two other individuals standing by and they chimed in, saying "Yeah, ours too." Everybody laughed, including her, then went on with our business. Yesterday I received notice of a complaint being lodged against me.

2. Military Dependents: National Origin

    Complainant: Female Dependent Oriental

    Offender: Female Dependent Black

    Complainant: We bowl every Friday night. I'm on a bowling team with three other ladies from Korea and Thailand. There is a Black lady on one of the other teams who continually talks about us. She calls us names and stares at us the whole time we are bowling. She slapped her husband one night because he was talking to me about Korea. She told me that she didn't want me nowhere near her husband. I don't know him and didn't start the conversation that night. I don't mind the stares so much, but I get embarrassed at the way she talks about us. I reported her to the manager at the bowling alley, but he said there was nothing he could do. My husband is in the Navy and has been at sea for five months so he can't help me. The lady says we have no right to bowl in the Air Force bowling alley, but the rule only states that we be military dependents to join the league. I want her to stop talking about me and stop staring at me. Can you help?

3. Racism Complaint

    Complainant: Black male SSgt

    Offender: SSgt Marine

    Complainant: I went into the Marine enlisted club looking to have a beer and cool off. This Marine sitting at the bar began to stare at me. I ordered a drink and some chips and began to watch TV at the bar. The Marine SSgt made a comment that I should use the Air Force club; they usually cater to my kind. I tried to ignore him, but he continued to make racial slurs directed at me. The bartender tried to quiet him down without success. Finally, I reported him to the night manager. They appeared to know each other well. Finally the guy left. The night manager informed me there might be trouble if I left by the front entrance and suggested I leave by a side door. I decided to have another drink and left by the front door. The SSgt was waiting and we got into a fight. The police arrested both of us, releasing me to my commander. I want you to get the Marine charged with racial prejudice and get my record wiped clean.

4.   Commander Religion

Complainant: 1st Lt Female

Offender: Lt Col Male

Complainant: I have a young 1st Lt female assigned to my unit who said she was going to lodge a complaint against me. She claims I will not allow her an opportunity to participate in various religious activities involving her church. The 1st Lt is an excellent musician I'm told and is in charge of her church choir. She claims that I've prevented her from attending various functions by changing her shift schedules. The 1st Lt is one of three officers assigned to the unit. We are required to have one officer on call each night ready to respond at a moment's notice. The 1st Lt, aside from being the newest member on board, single, and living on base, was recently trained on some delicate equipment, which one other officer is TDY receiving training for. Prior to her arrival, duties were covered by my two male officers. With one being TDY, I felt the 1st Lt must shoulder a larger role of responsibility. My remaining Captain has long been involved in some off-duty education and is nearing completion. I do not feel I should hinder him in his endeavors at this time. The problem will be resolved within two months with the return of the Captain who is TDY and the completion of the second Captain's education. I feel my actions are correct based on the circumstances. How can I prevent her from filing an EOT complaint against me?

5.   Racism Complaint

Complainant: Black Male Sgt

Offender: White Male TSgt

Complainant: Three days ago, I was involved in a name-calling incident with one of the guys in my dorm. He called me a name, I called him a name, we both went into our rooms, and that ended it. Last night, a TSgt came into the dorm looking for the guy I previously had the name-calling incident with. I came out of my door as he was going by. The TSgt asked me if I knew where the other guy lived. I said, "Yeah, down the hall." The TSgt asked me to show him the room. I said I was in a hurry and really didn't want to have anything to do with the guy. The TSgt insisted by grabbing me by the arm. I jerked my arm back telling him not to grab me. At that time the AMN I'd had the problem with stuck his head outside the door and yelled, "Sarge that's the [expletive] I was telling you about. He's always starting trouble." I yelled back at him, saying he should mind his own business. The TSgt said he'd handle this dumb [expletive]. Based on the TSgt's statement about the incident I received a letter of reprimand for insubordination. I want the letter of reprimand withdrawn and the TSgt cited for prejudice. Can you help me?

6. Sexual Discrimination by Supervisor
   Complainant: Female Security Policeman
   Offender: Male Supervisor

   Complainant: In October, I was called into my supervisor's office and informed that my application for dog handler training was being disapproved. I had previously applied for this training three months prior. At the time I applied, two other males requested the same training. The three of us have approximately the same time in service, the same rank, and experience as security police. I am friends with the two males and was informed by them that their applications were approved at base level and sent forward to the commander with recommendation for approval. My supervisor informed me that my application was disapproved in the squadron because they did not feel I was strong enough to control a dog. He further stated that in their opinion I had shown an abnormal fear of large dogs and possibly would wash out of school because of this. The supervisor could have only gotten this information through conversation with one of the other applicants. He has never observed me around animals. I've got a good working relationship with the supervisors and most of the people in the section. I don't want to ruin it. I would like a shot at the school, but I don't want to cause trouble in the squadron. What should I do?

7. Sexual Harassment
   Complainant: White Female (Military)
   Offenders: Two Civilian Contractors

   Complainant: They are painting some empty houses on my street. Since I live on base I go home for lunch each day. When I get out of my car they will usually come to the door of the house they are painting and whistle or yell at me. I have reported them, but nothing has come of it. I want them to leave me alone and if possible have the contractor thrown off base for not taking action. What should I do?

4.3
Case Studies: Critical Incidents With International Students

The objective of the following critical incident case examples (Brislin et al., 1986) is to encourage a group to identify and discuss the consequences of alternatives faced by international students. You will be presented with a series of situations that have actually happened to international students. You or a resource person should "take on the role" of the international student in each situation as though you or the resource person were experiencing the situation. A discussion guide is provided for each critical incident to help you judge responses "in role." You may choose to role-play the situation in front of a group with yourself in the role of the international student and others in the group seeking to "help you," to make the situation more realistic. If international students can be brought into the group as resource persons, your analysis and discussion are likely to be much more useful.

The international student resource person should be allowed to select an incident with which he or she is already familiar and comfortable. The more time the resource person has to consider the incident, the more realistic the student will be in projecting her- or himself into the role. The facilitator might ask the student to come to the front of the room while the facilitator briefly reads or summarizes the situation. The student is then invited to speak for 1 or 2 minutes about how he or she feels in that dilemma. Then the audience is invited to ask questions, give advice, comment, or respond to the student in some helpful way. After about 8 or 10 minutes, the facilitator ends the discussion. The resource person then goes out of the role and highlights those comments from the audience that seemed particularly helpful. Then the resource person is applauded, and the next resource person is introduced.

The Faculty Adviser

You came to the international student counselor for help on academic problems. It soon became apparent that you are having a difficult time communicating with your academic faculty adviser. You describe the adviser as always busy and as impatient with your questions when you did ask for clarification. As a result, you often agreed to decisions you did not really understand because you felt your adviser wanted you to answer that way. You are terrified of the academic adviser. The adviser is totally unaware of your feelings, and since you seldom sought him out for help, he assumed you are doing fine. You are your academic adviser's only international student advisee. Usually, international students are advised by two other faculty members in the department who are already overloaded with advisees. You want to change advisers to one of these other two faculty members who are too busy to accept new advisees.

Background

There is probably no relationship as important to the academic success of an international student as the relationship with his or her academic adviser. The adviser helps any student make the necessary decisions and adjustments, but this resource is particularly important for an international student who lacks the support system available to other students who have grown up in this country. Advisers often perceive international students as more time-consuming than U.S. nationals because international students are perceived to have greater difficulty in making adjustments. There are no extrinsic rewards in most university systems for faculty advisers who spend a lot of time working with international students and take their responsibility seriously. Some faculty seem to enjoy working with international students, however, and tend to accumulate more foreign students among their advisees than others. When a student has an unsatisfactory relationship with his or her faculty adviser, there is a formal procedure for changing advisers, but frequently the international student is unfamiliar with the procedure and embarrassed to make the change. Asking the student to change advisers can also be perceived as dangerous, in view of the academic adviser's fairly arbitrary authority and informal influence over other faculty members in the department.

The Actual Decision

The student was not forced to reject her academic adviser but was assigned one of the other faculty as a co-adviser along with her previous academic adviser. The previous academic adviser was able to learn more about the special problems in advising international students from his colleague who was more familiar with international students. The new co-advising faculty member was able to accept a share of the advising responsibility with a minimum of additional effort. The problem was solved without creating stereotyped "international student experts" among the faculty while at the same time training other faculty in the department to work with international students. Because all persons were spared an embarrassing confrontation, the student felt more confident that none of the faculty would be angry at her and prejudice her academic future.

Discussion Questions

1. Should some faculty specialize in advising international students?

2. Does advising international students require more effort than advising U.S. nationals?

3. When a student asks his or her adviser permission to change to another adviser, does the old adviser take this as a personal insult?

4. What are some of the special problems that come up in advising international students?

5. Why does the academic system not provide rewards for good advising as it does for good teaching and research?

Working Without Permission

You were caught working illegally by the Immigration and Naturalization Service (INS) and called to a deportation hearing. You claimed that you applied for work permission during the academic year but did not hear from the INS for two months. When summer came, you thought that international students were allowed to work without permission since they do not need to be in school. However, the INS claimed that you knew accepting the job was illegal, or you would not have applied for permission to work. Since you had never received a denial letter you felt the INS was being unfair. The procedure was lengthy and humiliating for you. You felt whatever offense might have been committed did not justify the expense of time and effort by either the INS or yourself. The job you took was in a nursing home for a small amount of pay after they had tried desperately but unsuccessfully to find someone else to work there. Finally, the INS relented and let you stay, but they gave you a scolding about the problems this country is facing with unemployment and made it plain that international students should never displace U.S. nationals. You listened to the lecture but felt bitter about it.

Background

The INS has tended to interpret regulations more strictly in recent years, particularly relating to an international student's financial support. The international student is subject to INS regulations, which are interpreted administratively without the due protection afforded under the law. From the student's point of view, the INS seems to be arbitrary in interpreting these regulations according to their feelings about particular students from particular countries. International students are easily intimidated by the INS, and even routine inquiries are often perceived as harassment. INS officers are not trained in cross-cultural communication beyond what they learn on the job. Consequently, their way of dealing with international students is not always sensitive to cultural variables. The regulations for international students staying temporarily in this country are both necessary and complicated. For exactly those reasons, it is especially important that INS staff have the benefit of some cross-cultural training. Many of their encounters with international students leave the students feeling as if they are suspected of committing a crime. Some of the students come from countries in which the "routine investigations" by government officials are perceived as police surveillance. There is probably no single aspect of an international student's U.S. experience as typically anxiety-provoking as staying in status with the INS. This puts a great burden of responsibility on the international student adviser both to know the regulations and to develop trusting relationships with INS agents and to help train INS staff where that opportunity is available.

The Actual Decision

Not all INS agents are insensitive. Most international student advisers have cultivated a relationship with at least one or two INS agents who are sensitive to international students' special circumstances and who take extra time to help international students through the system. In this case, the student was reassigned to a different and more sympathetic INS agent who helped the student understand the procedures for keeping the job and staying in status.

Discussion Questions

1. What are some reasons an international student might fear the INS?
2. Who would the INS describe as a "good" international student?
3. Under what conditions should international students be allowed to work while they are in the United States?
4. How will the student describe the INS to other international students?
5. How could trust between the INS and international students be encouraged?

"Fair" Grading

You asked the international student adviser to "talk to" your instructor to see if there was any way your grade in a particular course could be raised to a C. You believed you knew the material even though you did badly on the exam. You are already on probation, so a failing grade would cause the university to drop you. As a consequence, the INS would require you to return home or transfer to another program of study. Because it is in the middle of the year, no other university or program would be likely to accept transfers, especially from a failing student. After seeing both the faculty member and you, the adviser arranged a meeting for the three of you in the faculty member's office to identify alternatives.

From your point of view, the issue should be whether or not you know the material rather than how well adjusted you are to the U.S. environment. The adviser seemed intimidated by the system and unable to advocate your case as you would have liked.

Background

International students are at a disadvantage when competing with U.S. students for higher grades. U.S. students are accustomed to the grading system, familiar with the test format and questions, more fluent in English, not confronted by the multitude of cultural adjustments, and not subject to INS requirements that complicate an international student's life. Although these factors are not directly related to the student's academic performance, they certainly have an effect. Some well-meaning faculty who are aware of this inequity attempt to compensate for it by giving the international student higher grades than their work would ordinarily merit. Other international students sometimes use this argument in trying to get their grades changed. Other faculty feel they have no choice but to hold all their students accountable for the same level of academic achievement. The international student adviser is often asked to intervene on behalf of an international student when extenuating circumstances may have contributed to the student's failure. Not only the student but the university has a considerable investment to protect in helping the student succeed.

The Actual Decision

Ideally, the student should have been helped before he was put on probation, but frequently the student will avoid counseling except as a last resort. After some discussion, the faculty member agreed to let the student withdraw from the course retroactively, providing that the student would take more courses in English as a Second Language before continuing in the graduate program. The international student adviser met with the student to arrange a contract indicating in detail what the student had to do to stay in school, including regular meetings with the academic adviser. Being able to influence a policy decision also gave the international student adviser more confidence in his ability to work with the system.

Discussion Questions

1. Did this international student get more help than a U.S. student might have received under similar circumstances?
2. Should international students receive "special treatment" in helping them adjust to university requirements?
3. What were the other alternatives that could have resulted from this incident, and what were their consequences?
4. Why do you suppose the student didn't seek help earlier than he did?
5. Will the academic adviser get a reputation of being "soft" on international students for what he did?

The International Student Office

You are a U.S. student who wrote a letter to the campus newspaper suggesting that the International Student Office be eliminated. You wrote, "If we have to save money and cut budgets in the university, the least painful way is to abolish the position of the International Student Adviser and the supporting budget. For one thing, we cannot really maintain a separate office for a relatively small group of students. The time has come that we must treat all students alike and not have services for any 'special' group. Secondly, we really will not hurt anybody by this decision, because international students are just students like any other student and thus can enjoy the same services as are available to any other student. This action might actually work better for international students because having a special international student adviser probably isolates international students from other students. International students will be more integrated with other students on campus. The great majority of international students on our large campus reportedly don't visit the ISO office anyway unless they have to. It is only a small minority of international students that have difficulties and they are often marginal students who possibly should not have been brought here to begin with. We must make sure that these students make a realistic decision about leaving here if they can't make it on their own. The International Student Adviser's office often protects these students, asking for more and more exceptions when in fact these extensions only delay a decision to terminate them eventually. The money we save by eliminating the ISO can be redirected to important programs related to the special problems of our own society."

Background

The International Student Office was organized on most university campuses because of specialized problems arising among international students requiring specialized knowledge. To some extent, each campus office is designed as its own "Office of Student Affairs" for international students, with financial aid, housing, counseling, and other services being available. Problems of special immigration forms, difficulties in cross-cultural adjustment, and special requirements that international students need to meet prompted setting up this special office. The task of this office is loosely defined according to the needs of the international student population. Other special populations, such as ethnic minorities, have objected to the idea of an International Student Office as favoring one special group at the expense of other groups. If the office were eliminated, many of its services would be eliminated or shifted to other offices where staff would need to be retrained to perform them.

The Actual Decision

Eliminating the International Student Office was considered one way to streamline student services, but the office was retained. The objectives of the office were clarified, redefined, and specified in such a way that its contribution to the educational mission of the university was both obvious and necessary. The office responsibilities were changed from being a "service station" to a formal unit of academic affairs, helping to internationalize the formal and

nonformal university curriculum. Support groups were established for international students and U.S. nationals to work together in a structured setting. International students were invited to speak on the campus radio station about world events. International students were also assigned to speak at high schools throughout the community as resource persons. The role of the office was judged to be fundamental to the university mission.

Discussion Questions	1. Should there be a separate office on campus for international students?
	2. Would other offices be able to assume the responsibility of working with international students if the ISO office were eliminated?
	3. What are the weaknesses in the assumptions made by the letter's author to the university newspaper?
	4. How would you respond to international students who read this letter and came in to talk about it?
	5. What parts of the letter are true?

Financial Aid

You were refused financial aid and made an appointment with the Director of Financial Aid to learn why. You were told there was barely enough money to meet the needs of U.S. minorities such as Blacks, Native Americans, and Hispanics, whose needs came first. You became angry because international students were being evaluated by a more strictly defined need criteria than other students. You came to the international student adviser and said the reason why minorities were getting aid was their militancy and organizational pressure. You described this policy as part of an antiforeign bias in admissions, awarding teaching or research assistantships, and at every other point where international students always came last. You threatened to organize international students to demonstrate against the university. You complained that international students are being treated unfairly and inequitably. You asked the international student adviser to decide which side he is on, the students' or the institution's.

Background

Financial aid is usually allocated according to need rather than as a reward for academic excellence. It is, however, difficult to measure need across different individuals applying for assistance and even more difficult to compare the need of a U.S. national with that of an international student from another country. International students are not eligible for federal aid and are excluded from other programs available to U.S. nationals. Consequently, there is more pressure on those funds that are available to international students as well as other students generally. Financial problems have increased because of rising tuition and a diminished opportunity to work on or off campus. As a result, there are fewer funds but increased need for financial aid among students generally and among international students in particular. International students do not have local family resources, are often hampered by currency regulations against getting money from home, cannot drop out and work for a term without endangering their legal status, and are often unaware of those financial resources available to them. It is important that the international student adviser be somehow independent, even from the university he or she represents, to best serve the university. At the same time, the adviser must be *more* than an advocate of international student interests.

The Actual Decision

The international student adviser offered to help the student document the student's arguments with as many specific incidents of inequity as possible. They prepared a detailed plan on how specific policies could be made more equitable and requested that the report be placed on the agenda for the next Board of Regents meeting. The adviser suggested to the student that a public demonstration should only be a last resort after all normal channels for grievance failed to produce results.

Discussion Questions

1. Is financial assistance distributed equitably to international students in comparison with other student populations?
2. Should the international student adviser take the side of the university or that of the international student?
3. Is the office of the international student adviser fairly described as a buffer between students and the institution?
4. Would a demonstration be more effective than a report to the regents in changing policy?
5. Were the students being unreasonable in their demands for a review of the financial aid policy?

From Pedersen (1994).

□

4.4
Critical Incidents
in Tourist Groups

Objective   Use the Cultural Grid to identify responses appropriate for these critical incident examples of intercultural interaction in a host culture.

Instruction   Although the critical incidents cited below provide examples of incidents suitable for the four competency areas, they overlap with one another to a considerable degree. Whenever possible, critical incidents should be drawn from the participant's own intercultural experiences or experiences he/she is likely to have in the future. Write out your response to each incident and then review the guidelines from Unit 4.1 or 4.2 to measure your own intercultural skill.

I.   To understand the contributions and lifestyles of various racial cultural and economic groups in our society

1.   You are acquainted with a student whose lifestyle does not emphasize "time consciousness." The student's failure to meet deadlines had downgraded his otherwise adequate assignments and alienated the student from his teachers. Neither the school nor the student seem willing to adapt their style to one another. The student's father asks you what to do.

2.   You find that the inhabitants of a small village where you are staying resent Americans a great deal because of previous bad experiences with the U.S. military and tourists. You discover that you have been grossly overcharged at your hotel and taken advantage of in other ways. Your plan was to spend the whole summer in one place rather than tour around so that you would get to know the people and not be an ordinary "tourist." Now

you find they are taking out their hostility toward "Americans" on you as an individual. You seek the advice of a casual friend who seems better accepted by the people than yourself.

3. The person with whom you are traveling, a friend from back home, seems to be turning into an "Ugly American." He is condescending in his treatment of others, suspicious that he is being cheated, concerned that nothing is "clean" enough, and generally obnoxious toward non-Americans. You want to help him make a better adjustment both for his sake and because his behavior is embarrassing. You take him aside for a "little talk."

II. To recognize and deal with dehumanizing biases, discrimination, and prejudices

1. You are in a mixed group of new acquaintances. The elections have just been held with the political parties divided according to Protestant and Roman Catholic lines. The discussion is extremely intense and likely to erupt into violence. You are not well enough acquainted with the issues to recognize which of the persons in your group belong to which political party and/or which religious group. One of the leaders in the group asks you for your opinion.

2. In becoming acquainted with your host family you discover that the women in this society are in a very subservient role, having to work very hard and being completely dominated by men. Cautious inquiries suggest that this style of life is well accepted and normal even though it seems extremely unfair to you as a woman. Your anger over this unfair treatment is beginning to show, and the members of your host family are starting to make fun of you for being a "women's lib" type.

3. In spite of your best efforts in learning the foreign language, you find yourself very inadequate in your ability to express yourself. The persons with whom you talk on the street seem very impatient and somewhat irritated by the way you do violence to their language. You refuse to use English, even though their English is very adequate, but you are beginning to resent their lack of sympathy with your attempts to enter their culture. You catch yourself becoming unreasonably angry with a complete stranger who doesn't understand you when you ask him a simple question.

III. To create learning environments that contribute to the self-esteem of all persons and to positive interpersonal relations

1. You are Jewish and find yourself in a large German city where everyone seems prejudiced against you. You had many relatives who suffered under the Germans in concentration camps but you were never aware of any strong anti-German bias until now. It

seems impossible to separate your feelings against them as a group from your relationship with them as individuals. You can understand and explain your bias but you cannot seem to control your feelings which are coming out in your behavior toward Germans. A German casual acquaintance asks you if you are Jewish since you "look" Jewish and you become extremely angry with him.

2. You are Black and have been invited to speak before a class of secondary students who have never seen or talked with a Black. A friend of yours invited you to come and explain to them about the racial problem in the United States and what is being done to combat racism.

3. The leader of your group is a very authoritarian male who succeeds in dominating, planning, and controlling the activities of the group. He is very jealous of any threat to his control. Other members of the group are able to tolerate his domination, but you find it increasingly impossible. The other group members have begun looking to you, a woman with considerable international experience, for advice and guidance on what to do. You believe that the leader is doing a bad job and resents your threat to his authority. You sit down to "have it out" with him for the sake of the group as well as yourself.

IV. Respect human diversity and personal rights

1. One of your friends is planning to marry a foreign national who is of a different religion as well as a different nationality. Neither set of parents agrees to the marriage, and the engaged couple is not sure they will be able to overcome the differences of culture and of religion. At the same time they are unwilling to separate and are hopeful that once they are married their families will somehow come to agree. They ask your advice.

2. Your new friends insist on borrowing things from you and neglect to return them unless you ask for them back. They appear much more casual about "ownership" of personal belongings than you would like and assume that they have a right to your things as your friends. You try to set an example by not borrowing anything from them, but they continue to borrow from you and don't acknowledge the subtle hints you make. They seem to be using you to their own advantage, although among themselves they seem to have developed a satisfactory arrangement.

3. You have been caught with a group of friends who were in possession of marijuana. The police have placed all of you in jail and are not allowing you to contact anyone outside the jail. The conditions are impossible, and you feel that you are entirely at the mercy of the jailer. You are ready to do just about anything to get out of the jail and are angry since you didn't even break the law in the first place. You need to find some way to get help.

4.5
Critical Incidents
in Airline Travel

Objective   Identify the barriers to intercultural communication in these intercultural situations about airline travel.

Instructions   The following eight situations that occurred aboard an international airline were collected to illustrate the dynamics of intercultural communication for a training program.

Read each situation, the points of view of the people involved, and then a list of actual intercultural communication barriers encountered aboard the airline. Match each of these with one or more of the five intercultural communication barriers discussed in Unit 4.2. An answer key appears at the bottom of each situation page.

Key   Pax = passenger
F/A = flight attendant
Barriers = 1 = language, 2 = stereotyping, 3 = evaluation,
                     4 = nonverbal, 5 = stress

SITUATION 1: "Last Rites" (Latin American pax/U.S. pax/U.S. F/A)

As each of the pax boarded the plane, a new F/A noticed that several Latin American Pax crossed themselves and seemed to say a small prayer as though they were expecting to crash and were preparing to die. When one of the U.S. pax called the F/A's attention to this behavior and asked what it meant, the F/A was not sure enough of the accurate interpretation to respond, even though the F/A felt it was his responsibility to respond in some way.

From the Latin Americans' perspective, they were practicing their religious beliefs as they had learned them to provide comfort in a stressful or unfamiliar situation.

From the U.S. pax perspective, there was some suspicion associated with a group of persons speaking a "foreign" language and performing an unfamiliar ritual.

From the F/A's perspective, he was having to explain a cultural behavior when he didn't really know the answer.

Match the barriers with the five ICC categories:

a. __ use of a foreign language

b. __ religious beliefs that seem strange to some and familiar to others

c. __ expectations of foreigners being suspicious

d. __ coping with a situation in an unfamiliar way

e. __ making an unfamiliar gesture with ambiguous meaning

Answers: (a) 1 (b) 2 (c) 2, 3 (d) 5 (e) 4

SITUATION 2: "A Money Tip" (Middle Eastern pax/U.S. F/A)

During one flight through the Middle East, one wealthy Middle Eastern pax was very pleased with the service received from the F/A and wanted to show his appreciation. As the flight was preparing to land, he handed the F/A a sealed envelope and asked the F/A not to open the envelop until she had reached her hotel that night. The F/A agreed not to open the envelop and accepted his explanation that it was a card with a poem of appreciation in it, which would be embarrassing if the F/A opened it in his presence. When the F/A opened the envelope later, she discovered that it contained a large amount of money.

From the Middle Eastern pax viewpoint, he was used to giving a gift of appreciation for special occasions and to have the gift rejected would be a serious insult to him.

From the F/A's point of view, it is not according to regulations to accept money gifts, but she doesn't want to offend the pax either and she would like to keep the money.

Match the barriers with the five ICC categories:

a. __ the money itself and all it symbolizes

b. __ the possible expectation that the pax might want special favors

c. __ the airline regulations prohibiting both accepting money and offending pax

d. __ the Middle Eastern customs about giving and receiving gifts

e. __ anxiety in wanting to please both the airlines and the pax

Answers: (a) 4 (b) 2, 3 (c) 3, 5 (d) 2, 4 (e) 5

SITUATION 3: "Left-Handed F/A" (Middle Eastern pax/U.S. F/A)

One of the F/As happens to be left-handed and normally uses her left hand in whatever task she performs. On one flight, a Middle Eastern pax in First Class became extremely upset when the F/A served him his drink with the left hand and refused to accept the service. Furthermore, the pax insisted on filing a formal complaint against the F/A for being extremely insulting and failing to acquaint herself with Middle Eastern customs.

The Middle Eastern pax expected the F/A to know some of their customs since they fly to that part of the world and was insulted when the F/A used her left hand, which is considered both ritually and literally unclean in Middle Eastern culture.

The F/A did not understand what she had done wrong and saw herself as treating all the pax alike, so if the rest of the pax were happy with the service, why should the Middle Eastern pax be unhappy?

Match the barriers with the five ICC categories:

a. __ Middle Eastern customs about the left hand being unclean

b. __ The pax's expectations of F/As being knowledgeable

c. __ The F/A's habit of using her left hand

d. __ The anger of the Middle Eastern pax

e. __ Stress at having made the Middle Eastern pax angry enough to write a complaint letter

Answers: (a) 1, 3 (b) 2 (c) 4 (d) 5 (e) 3, 5

SITUATION 4: "Finger Snapping" (Latin American pax/U.S. F/A)

A well-dressed and quite wealthy Latin American male was sitting in the First Class section, demanding special attention from the F/A. He would call for the F/A by snapping his fingers repeatedly until she turned around and came over to his seat. The F/A had experienced more than enough difficulty during the day and was getting irritated at his calling by snapping his fingers.

From the Latin American pax point of view, he was calling for service as he would call for any servant back home and requiring only the courtesies due him from those of lesser rank in society.

From the F/A's viewpoint, his snapping his fingers was demeaning and offensive to the extreme and suggested his wanting immediate and very special attention beyond the attention given to other pax.

Match the barriers with the five ICC categories:

a. __ snapping fingers as a mode of asking for service

b. __ a superior attitude toward inferior ranks of society

c. __ anger at being looked down upon

d. __ stereotypes of servants to include F/As

e. __ unwillingness to adapt to other forms of calling for service, like using the call button

Answers: (a) 4 (b) 2, 3 (c) 5 (d) 3 (e) 2, 4

SITUATION 5: "European Style" (European F/A/U.S. F/A)

One of the European F/As was being criticized by the other F/As for being blunt and discourteous in her treatment of the pax and in her relations with other F/As. When the European was confronted with this criticism, she saw herself as being appropriately formal in her relationships according to the guidelines of professional behavior. She interpreted any less formal behaviors as unprofessional. Several of the U.S. F/As are discussing ways of dealing with this difference of opinion.

From the European F/A's point of view, she should be allowed to conduct her work independently in a formal and professional style as she had learned from her culture without interference from coworkers.

From the U.S. F/As' point of view, it is necessary to be informal and friendly to all pax and for all other F/As from other cultures to work together as a team on that basis.

Match the barriers with the five ICC categories:

a. __ the learned meaning of professional behavior

b. __ the interpretation of formal behavior as unfriendly

c. __ isolation of a culturally different coworker F/A

d. __ stereotypes of pax reaction to formal behavior by a F/A

e. __ giving negative feedback to a coworker from another culture

Answers: (a) 2 (b) 4 (c) 3 (d) 2 (e) 3

SITUATION 6: "Everybody Looks Alike" (Asian F/A/U.S. pax)

A U.S. pax called one of the Asian F/As and asked that her bag be returned to her. The Asian F/A insisted that she had not taken the woman's bag, but the pax became more and more angry, insisting that the Asian F/A was lying. At this point, one of the other Asian F/As came up to the woman and volunteered that she had been the F/A who had stored the woman's bag and would get it immediately. The U.S. pax excused herself, saying that all Orientals look alike anyway.

From the U.S. pax's point of view, she was a bit suspicious of the foreign F/As and was anxious that she not be taken advantage of in any way.

From the F/A's point of view, they were being unfairly stereotyped as all alike just because they were from a different culture and not being treated as individuals.

Match the barriers with the five ICC categories:

a. __ the stereotyped expectation about Asian F/As

b. __ the pax's anger at believing she was being lied to by the F/A

c. __ the embarrassment by both pax and F/As

d. __ the similarity between the two Asian F/As

e. __ the pax's anxiety about her bag

Answers: (a) 2 (b) 3, 5 (c) 3, 5 (d) 2 (e) 5

SITUATION 7: "Knife, Fork, and Spoon" (Asian pax/U.S. pax/U.S. F/A)

The very traditional Asian pax was obviously uncomfortable during the meal service and was not touching any of the food. The pax had indicated earlier that she was very hungry, so the F/A was surprised when the F/A picked up her full tray at the end of the meal service. Later, the person sitting next to the Asian pax talked with the F/A and confided that the pax did not eat, even though she was hungry, because she was not used to using a knife and fork but preferred chopsticks.

The Asian pax wanted to avoid an embarrassing situation by either asking for chopsticks or trying to eat with a knife and fork and doing it improperly, so she chose to withdraw.

The F/A did not know that the Asian pax preferred chopsticks and served her the way she had served all the other pax, assuming that all pax would prefer knives and forks.

Match the barriers with the four ICC categories:

a. __ the unfamiliar custom of eating with a knife, fork, and spoon

b. __ the embarrassment of requiring special attention

c. __ the expectation that all pax eat with a knife and fork and spoon

d. __ the lack of fluency in English by the pax or in Japanese by the F/A

Answers: (a) 4 (b) 3, 5 (c) 2, 3 (d) 1

SITUATION 8: "Saying Yes or No" (Asian pax/U.S. F/A)

An Asian pax, who did not speak English, was flying alone and was shy among so many strangers. The F/A was trying to help the Asian pax be more comfortable, but every time the F/A would ask her a question the Asian pax would shake her head up and down as though saying "yes" while moving her open palm from side to side in front of her face as though saying "no." The more the F/A tried to interpret her gesture, the more embarrassed and uncomfortable the Asian pax became.

From the Asian pax's point of view, she is more interested in reducing embarrassment than getting service and is trying to respond appropriately in a neutral way that leaves the decision up to the F/A for interpretation.

From the U.S. F/A's viewpoint, she is trying to get a simple yes or no answer from the pax so she can get on with the job of providing service and is determined to get a response without regard for the embarrassment that results.

Match the barriers with the five ICC categories:

a. __ the ambiguous hand signal

b. __ the expectation that the pax wants service

c. __ the method of saying yes or no to a question

d. __ anxiety at flying by herself

e. __ the embarrassment of not being able to respond appropriately as the F/A expects a pax should respond

Answers: (a) 4 (b) 2 (c) 1 (d) 5 (e) 2, 5

Sources Consulted

Albert, R. D. (1983). The intercultural sensitizer or culture assimilator: A cognitive approach. In D. Landis & R. W. Brislin, *Handbook of intercultural training: Volume 2. Issues in training methodology* (pp. 186-217). New York: Pergamon.

Brislin, R. W., Cushner, K., Cherrie, C., & Yong, M. (1986). *Intercultural interactions: A practical guide.* Beverly Hills, CA: Sage.

Fiedler, F. E., Mitchell, T. R., & Triandis, H. C. (1971). The culture assimilator: An approach to cross-cultural training. *Journal of Applied Psychology, 55*, 95-102.

Fivars, G. (1980). *The critical incident technique: A bibliography.* Palo Alto, CA: American Institutes for Research.

Flanagan, J. C., & Burns, R. K. (1955). The employee performance record: A new appraisal and development tool. *Harvard Business Review, 33*(5), 95-102.

Freire, P. (1993). *Pedagogy of the oppressed.* Trans. Myra Ramos.

Moran, R. T., Westerhauser, J. A., and Pedersen, P. B. (1974). *Dress rehearsal for a cross-cultural experience.* International Educational and Cultural Exchange.

Pedersen, P. (1994). International students and international student advisers. In R. B. Brislin & T. Yoshida, *Improving intercultural interactions* (pp. 1148-1170). Newbury Park, CA: Sage.

Pedersen, P. B. (1995). *The five stages of culture shock: Critical incidents around the world.* West Port, CT: Greenwood.

Porter, J. W. and Haller, A. D. (1962). *Michigan international student problem inventory.* East Lansing, MI: International Programs.

Sauser, W. I. (1987). Critical incident technique. In R. Corsini (Ed.), *Concise encyclopedia of psychology* (p. 272). New York: John Wiley.

Sue, D. W., & Sue, D. (1990). *Counseling the culturally different: Theory and practice* (2nd ed.). New York: John Wiley.

Thielen, H. A. (1993). *Dynamic of groups at work*. Chicago: University of Chicago.

Weeks, W., Pedersen, P., & Brislin, R. (1977). *A manual of structured experiences for cross-cultural learning*. Yarmouth, ME: Intercultural.